MARIAN CHRISTY'S CONVERSATIONS

Marian Christy's Conversations

Famous Women Speak Out

Courage,
Marian Christy

Marian Christy

Lumen Editions
a division of Brookline Books

ISBN 1-57129-061-3

Library of Congress Cataloging-In-Publication Data
Christy, Marian.
    Marian Christy's conversations : famous women speak out / by
Marian Christy.
        p.   cm.
    ISBN 1-57129-061-3 (pbk.)
    1. Women--Interviews. 2. Celebrities--Interviews. 3. Success-
-Psychological aspects. I. Title.
HQ1154.C49   1998
305.4--DC21   98-20030
                                                   CIP

Front cover design by Matthew Brock.
Book design and typography by Erica L. Schultz.

Printed in USA by Banta Book Group, Menasha, WI.
10 9 8 7 6 5 4 3 2 1

Published by
Lumen Editions
a division of Brookline Books
P.O. Box 1047
Cambridge, Massachusetts 02238
Order toll-free: 1-800-666-BOOK

Contents

In memory of my mother, Anna Christy,
and for Robert French with love

Acknowledgments

Thank you to Sadi Ranson, my brilliant editor, who made the journey with me.

Thank you to Dr. Howard Gotlieb, the Director of Special Collections at Boston University, who started collecting my papers a decade ago and on whose friendship, personal and professional, I have always relied. He has given it without fail.

Thank you to Alfred S. Larkin, Jr., Vice President of *The Boston Globe*, who gave me access to my interviews and stipulated that the only thank-you he expected was: "Reprinted courtesy of *The Boston Globe*."

Foreword

There are many famous women in this book. But they are the same woman.

You know her. She is Everywoman who has ever smashed into a roadblock—usually not of her own making—and, refusing to be barricaded, found an intensely personal way to make a molehill out of that mountain.

I met these luminaries by that chance encounter glibly referred to as "The Interview." As a newspaper journalist with a streak of independence, I purposely tossed aside what celebrities dismiss angrily as "those same damned questions." Instead I asked about specific matters of the soul.

"How did you tap into the strength of your own powers?"

"What did you do when things got tough?"

"Why didn't you retreat in panic? Weren't you scared?"

"What made you think you could get from where you were to where you wanted to be?"

Our professional celebrity-journalist relationship, measured in a set block of meticulously monitored minutes, was originally slotted for strictly promotional purposes. Yet somehow the exchange became magical. We were strangers. But "they" and "me" became "us." We forged a friendship that was of the moment, for the moment, and by the moment.

Moments, by their nature, are fleeting. The written word is not. I listened hard and wrote from the heart because what I shared with these intense women, and what I now share with you, were crystalline moments born of the wisdom of experience.

What burned these women into my consciousness is that they all spoke to me of their bouts with darkness within the context of light. The passive acceptance of the status quo—unfulfillment—was never an option. Something had to be done. So they gambled on their inner resources and did it their way. Using different words, they reduced their courage to its simplest component: the power of attitude.

What continues to keep me under their hypnotic spell is that the common chord that they sang solo is, in reality, Everywoman's Symphony. It goes like this: Stark self-appraisal leads to self-reliance which leads to self-empowerment.

Tyranny takes many forms. Each story is Everywoman: fiercely individual and personal. The same reward has many choruses. I am Everywoman too.

—M.C.

Prologue

The seed of this book was planted over a cup of tea when I was seventeen years old. Distance and time, mingled with experience, makes me believe that the better you know my beginnings, the better you will understand how my life became intertwined with the lives of the dazzling women who dance across this stage.

They had the guts and grit to deal with the many limitations of prefeminist existence. It was always on their own terms and by their own means. Their stories are as original as their fingerprints. What links them forever to you, and to me, is that they, too, sailed past the tricky straits of all kinds of secret STOP signs. They liberated themselves, and flourished, despite the confining tyrannies that were peculiar to the female species before feminism became a household world.

I had not asked to crash the Little League, attend West Point, sit on the Supreme Court or become the first woman Secretary of State. I was dying to go to college, to study how to communicate elegantly with the written word, and my father, the patriarch with the pocketbook, thought that the words I should put to paper did not go beyond that of an employed stenographer in a take-a-letter environment that he referred to as "clerking."

When, shaking in my penny loafers and bobby socks, I summoned the courage to beg him to help me go to college or junior college, or, at least, sanction the idea of daughter in college on her own, his indelible cutoff was a trail of brief condescending laughter. He knew a thousand ways to say no. They all hurt.

My father's rejection pushed me into a downward emotional spiral. My mother, the family's first prefeminist, knew that life in the doldrums was no life at all. She also knew that my father not only frowned on female progress, he banned it. Her antidote to all crises of this nature was for us to take a cup of tea together. The familiar ritual seemed especially inconsequential on the heels of the debilitating obstacles he thrust in his first daughter's career path. Sipping tea, though a ladylike and civilized gesture, was, I thought, tantamount to slowing down. But I humored my mother, the savant, not knowing that, in the grander scheme, she was humoring me.

One teatime melodrama changed forever the direction of my life and it began the way it had always begun. "Tea for two!" my mother sang sweetly in soprano.

I've always been amused that "our" song, my mother's and mine, hailed from the 1924 musical comedy, No No Nanette. Nanettes, who'd only gotten the right to vote in 1920, were still everywhere there was a No No involving equal rights.

The teas my mother orchestrated were the setting and excuse for compelling and indelible woman-to-woman talks about my assuming a penchant for positive thinking. Taking tea privately, just the two of us in the kitchen, was her way of using time to imbue me with a bright vision of myself. She wanted me to see me as I wanted to be—rather than the way I was.

I spoke of being stopped. My mother spoke of being unstoppable. I spoke of being without funds, of being unable to help myself to an education. "Just a temporary setback," she countered. I spoke of being lost. "There's always a way." I spoke of failure. She said failure was final only if I thought it was final. I said I'd lost my battle. She said I'd win my war. I spoke idealistically of equal opportunity. She said I'd pioneer my own opportunity.

I told her that she was nice and had taught me to be nice and that niceness now seemed to project a sense of not rocking the boat, of accepting the awful status quo, of bowing to gender subserviency. "Nice guys finish last," I said, making it sound like a crucifixion. And, quicker than the blink of an eye, she replied: "Nice guys finish *at last.*"

My mother was a patient woman. She viewed patience as a mark of low-key but unrelenting female determination. She also believed that a woman should fight for her rights without ever seeming to fight. Politeness, courtesy, good manners, and goodwill—even genuine kindness—were, she said, tools of communication. She spoke of women warriors but believed they need not forsake their womanly ways. I only half-listened. My anger was not yet channeled.

What stood between me and my dream of becoming a journalist was chauvinism. I was born into it. It was all I knew. The air around the house always ran heavy with strict admonishments and dire warnings that had a crippling connotation in a non-active verb that, to this day, I loathe.

That word is *cannot.*

You cannot learn to skate. You cannot have friends. You cannot go to any school dance. You cannot join the after-school French Club for star students. You cannot wait until June to graduate from high school because you must start work early in the spring. My father hurled "cannot" even when he found me off in a corner, quietly reading extracurricular literature suggested by one of my high school English teachers, Mr. Thomas Burns (who encouraged me to write dissertations which he actually took the time to grade), or even *Life* magazine. "You cannot read when there is housework," my father said about housework that was already done.

And, the worst, you cannot, cannot, cannot go to college spoken in those withering and patronizing hahaha's.

I succumbed, temporarily, to the idea that my desire to be a journalist was irrational. I was stymied financially and emotionally, beset with crippling self-doubts. I knew nothing about the world of newspapering which, of course, was another male bastion. Still I smoldered with desire to learn how to draw word pictures, to assume a voice that reached the ear by the eye. I not only wanted to earn a living—I wanted to make journalism my reason for living.

My mother used to say that I spoke with my eyes. She read the crushed feelings scrolled into my glance. She had movie-star good looks and was best-dressed before I knew what best-dressed meant and that money had nothing to do with it. She was a crack housekeeper, a chef who made gourmet meals out of budget food. She produced children and stood by her man even when it went against her grain. She honored and obeyed.

She was ahead of her time except in the divorce department. She viewed divorce as a social disgrace, a sin against the church. She spoke of marriage as an irrevocable contract, reminding me of her wedding oath: "Till death do us part." It was only after she became a widow that she confided that what kept her out of the divorce courts was my politically-connected father's continuing threat that he would, and could, get custody of the children. There were no women's rights then, especially in a court of law, and she did what she had to do. She was the wife who made a career out of motherhood.

But, in the secret passages of her heart and mind, she was a liberationist who empathized with my liberationist leanings. The woman who had given me life told me, over tea, that I could get a life. I had a clean slate, she said, an open road. During "that" tea, the one that changed my destiny, I asked her, *How?* How does a woman master her own fate? She, who could always put illuminating clues in the ordinary, bent the most clichéd of clichés to make her point comically: "Woman is the mother of invention."

Now, in hindsight, I see that the whimpers she and I made were prophetic of a burgeoning crescendo. Feminism was building up everywhere there was a mother like mine and a daughter like me. There were no mass marches then, no bra-burning follies and no mass information about birth control. There were no househusbands. No day-care centers. No equal opportunities in the workplace. There was no Oprah and no television forum to shock women into liberation-awareness. All women's struggles, and their many twists and turns, were hidden in the privacy of their lives. It was a man's world and, my God, we were sitting around a teapot talking about a woman, me, making good.

My mother also thought that wishing could make it so. I argued that blind faith isn't real. She countered that a woman of faith can make things happen if she blinds herself to obvious obstacles and applies her energy to a focused goal.

She also believed in the combined forces of ardent prayers, unrelentingly hard work, and a little luck. She was the most beautiful homefront soldier I've ever seen. I latched on to her simplistic homilies because I was drowning in doubt and she always projected the balm of hope. Her name was Anna. It was during that tea, when she defined her unelaborate "you can" concept, when she assured me that it was possible for a woman—any woman—to make a molehill out of a mountain, that I told her she should have been named Grace, as in Amazing Grace.

My father overheard us. We were talking emancipation talk. He pounced into the kitchen as silently and quickly as a tiger and accused my mother of teaching me to fight a "one-woman war." He called it self-defeating, hahaha.

No one yet knew then that self-empowerment, in the context of The Liberation Movement, would become every woman's salvation.

My father was disappointed that his firstborn was female. It was not unusual for him to refer to me as "her" or "she" rather than by name. Why would he acknowledge me otherwise when my feelings and opinions went unrecognized? I know for absolutely sure that it was my father's fanatical prejudice against educating me that left in its wake the first three letters of the most magical verb in the feminist dictionary: can.

All I knew then is that I wanted a chance. I didn't want to be thwarted and that river of desire ran so deep that it consumed my passivity. There would be no return to the prison of my own tentativeness, to what my father thought a woman should be: compliant for compliancy's sake. But I was a fledgling. I didn't know that this tentative brush with the inner strength of me is what modern feminists now call "attitude."

What probably had fascinated my father, what had stopped him in his tracks and maybe even threatened his stronghold on us, was my mother's detailed philosophy of what actually constituted a woman's "unstoppability."

Maybe it was the first time he had ever heard his wife talk that way: pointedly, uninhibitedly, confidently, spiritually, politically. Maybe he suspected she was talking back to him circuitously by talking to me in ways he had never imagined that women talked.

Now I see the everlasting eloquence of my mother's prefeminist reasoning.

She advocated that a woman break down a problem, any given problem, and devise a solution, not in one fell swoop, but by addressing each part of the whole. To gain ground, or take ground, little by little, has a cumulative effect. She had been talking to me about the power of organization and increasing one's impact with a series of small strategies that summarize the stuff of success.

On the clicking heels of my father's militaristic exit, my mother continued to talk, as if his words, designed to squelch us both, were a divine inspiration. She didn't consider his interruption a degradation of two women, mother and daughter, transformed by tea-taking into teacher and student. She continued to brainstorm a philosophy that had an underlying theme: freedom of expression, not only between ourselves, but for ourselves, and particularly in a bigger future reference for me.

She was, in that small moment of big connotations, as unstoppable as every woman in this book.

My mother spoke of women as graceful creatures who toughed things out with spiritual elegance. Remember, she said, that there was something innately powerful in being endowed, by nature, to produce a baby. She said that a woman's physical will, entrenched in the ability to see through the birthing travail, permeates her with an overall emotional strength of purpose that can have enormous impact on every dimension of her life.

A stark realist, especially when it came to me, she said that some women were destined to give birth to themselves, their dreams, their talents, their energies and their successes. If that was my choice, at least for that moment, she promised to back me.

She made it possible for me to fight my one-woman war.

Ginger Rogers

on pride

Ginger Rogers was immobilized in a wheelchair. Until the end of her days she was stuck in the stifling confines of the adult equivalent of a baby carriage.

Rogers, who was born in Independence, Missouri, first worked as a typist for a Kansas City mail-order house. Her pay was $9 a week. When "The Boys," a famous vaudeville team, needed a substitute, her friend Eddie Joy Jr., who had taught her how to do the Charleston, suggested that she fill in.

She accepted, and it turned out to be the first day of the rest of her career. After that, she got her own vaudeville contract, and by May, 1924, she was making $3,000 a week.

Now her magic feet were useless. Her body was bloated, probably from the terrible side effects of prescription drugs. She peered at me from behind oversized eyeglasses which covered the middle third of her face. She was eighty years old. This was one of her last hurrahs.

What crashed across my consciousness was the memory of my mother, also confined to a wheelchair, dying of the advanced stages of colon cancer, her time dwindling away. We communicated no longer in complete sentences. The disease had chomped on her brain. We spoke reams in a word here and there.

One of the last words my mother muttered to me was: "Proud!"

She meant she was proud of me. But it was she, stoic until the end, who made me proud to be her daughter. I whispered in my mother's ear that she was the author of my achievements. With great effort, she repeated herself, "Proud!", meaning she had nothing to do with it.

Ginger Rogers in a wheelchair. My mother in a wheelchair.

The pitiful twin images collided in my brain, merged and wouldn't go away.

My mother had hated the lowered position the wheelchair imposed on her. It diminished her like it diminishes all wheelchair-dependents. People automatically looked down at her. And she was forced to look up to whoever was standing around.

I made my own wheelchair rule about my mother.

Except when I was at the wheel and she couldn't see me anyway, I never, never stood. I sat on the floor. It was a symbolic gesture of our lifelong mutuality. But it was more than that. I wanted her to know that I would always, always look up to her, that she was my heroine. She patted my head. I understood that she understood.

Now Ginger Rogers was in the same straits.

Rogers peered up at me from behind those tinted oversized eye-glasses. She was waiting for me to react to the wheelchair, to her, to the planned interview.

I knew what I had to do. I sunk to the floor, yoga style. Interviews aren't just journalistic journeys. They're human journeys. They're emotional journeys. I asked Rogers, whom I was meeting for the first and only time: "What was the thing that made you most proud of yourself?"

"Proud?" she said, snatching the key word, "proud to be a Ms." There was no need to ask her to explain. Long before feminism was invented, before a woman could be called Ms., Rogers had liberated herself in Hollywood, in a world ruled only by studio dictators.

She said she was proud that no man had ever pushed her around. Not her five husbands. Not even Fred Astaire. What? The world has this indelible picture of Rogers, her magic feet crammed into the restrictive confines of high heels and, when the band played on, she floated like a whirling-twirling feather in Astaire's arms. She bent perfectly to his every dance floor whim and, in perfect harmony, they became the TwentiethCentury duo who memorialized terpsichorean splendor.

Reel life was not real life

Rogers had been galled to hear, via a grapevine rumor, that, without consulting her, Astaire had signed an agreement to release a dance segment they had done together in another film.

Astaire, the chauvinist, had refused to recognize theirs as a 50-50 partnership in the contracts department. Astaire had expected Rogers to bow silently to his maneuvers. When Ginger Rogers and Fred Astaire danced together, the partnership seemed to be the epitome of perfect harmony. But it wasn't always a case of perfect coordination. Rogers floated in trails of chiffon, but this soft exterior image didn't work when it came to dealing with Astaire on business matters.

Rogers had to fight for her rights, to be a feminist when feminism wasn't the fashion.

Rogers didn't sue Astaire. She confronted him in an environment of conviviality. She schemed with a mutual friend to home-cook an Italian meal for Astaire. When he was relaxed, guard down, she stepped on his toes.

Since I was sitting on the floor, I had a close-up of her feet. She lifted one up two or three inches and stamped it down to make her point about pride.

    I was angry. Someone told me that "someone" had given written permission to use a dance segment we had done together. At the dinner, I said to Astaire: "Did you give permission?"

He said: "Yes."

I said: "What do you think I am, your fifth leg?" I said: "How dare you do this without my approval?"

Astaire didn't apologize. But he never did anything like that again. After that, he was careful not to make too many demands. Occasionally he tested the waters and I reacted. After that, things got better.

In business relationships I had to be firm. If you're wishy-washy, down the drain you go. But I was always a clean fighter.

Sometimes I've had to compromise an issue raised by an opponent. But I stated my case—firmly. I never pounded on desk.

People tried to railroad me into doing movies I didn't want to do. It wasn't fun to follow the edicts of dictators. Sometimes I had to do as I was told.

My mother never stood in my way. She just said: "Go ahead and bump your head." She was talking about my choice of husbands. She'd say: "Your choice leaves a lot to be desired."

Every time I bought a house, I thought: "I'll be here forever with someone." That was never the case. My career never talked back to me. My husbands did. We had arguments. Lots of arguments. I loathed arguments.

I never would have considered just staying home and being a wife. I loved my work. The real joys I found always came from my work. I was born in a town called Independence. I'm independent. I've never wanted to feel locked up. To me, dancing symbolizes freedom.

When I danced in the studios, I thought I was outdoors, in the sunshine, in the fresh air. I was in a walled-in room. But I didn't feel walled-in. That was enough for me.

Just being onstage made me feel joyous. I never had felt so happy. I appeared in a school play my mother wrote. In the last scene, my "husband" is struck by an arrow and falls dead. I was to start crying as the curtain came down. I cried. I couldn't stop crying. My mother said: "The play is over. You can stop crying."

I said: "I can't stop because being there, on the stage, makes me feel so happy." And I cried some more.

Maya Angelou

on transcendence

Maya Angelou, the poet laureate, has lived a life marred by a series of unthinkable personal calamities. When she was seven, she became a voluntary mute. She had been raped.

Shortly after the invasion of her body and of her soul, she stopped talking for five years.

Silence is a fascinating subject as it applies to Angelou, one of the foremost communicators of our times. Her words could, but don't, come in snarls. She personifies soul peace and her inner light shines like a beacon.

I wanted to know where her anger went. Some survivors are forever angry. Who can blame them? Life whammed them hard. Not only did they have to survive, a solemn task in itself, but they also had to invent their own method of survival.

Why wasn't Angelou bubbling with rage?

Knowing some of the awful snippets of her personal history, which include homelessness and being stabbed by her father's lover, I told her that she must be a woman of many strengths. "You are exceptionally self-reliant," I said.

Angelou, being a writer-teacher, asked me what I thought self-reliance involved.

I told her my mother's theory and mine: that self-reliance involves a certain amount of acceptance. You have to acknowledge a situation for what it is, not what you wish it could have been.

My mother also believed, and I do, that any woman caught in a stranglehold has to imagine the solution to her freedom in terms of options, of choices, and believe that there's always more than one strategy at your disposal.

The word, *choices*, put exclamation points in Angelou's eyes. Words are Angelou's business. She sang the word *choices* several times, playing it like a gentle, caressing, harmonious Mozart chord.

"Choices! Choices! Choices!"

Then she got serious.

What, she asked, had my mother said about choices?

I told her that choice involves taking all the information you have at hand, doing what you think is right and never looking back. No second thoughts. My mother told me to hang onto the rightness of my choice. Hang tough. Hang alone. Hang no regrets on myself.

Angelou sang again. "Choices! Choices! Choices!" This chord, a variation of the theme, was louder, more emphatic.

Because she was born to rhyme, she added another word but reduced it to the singular of herself.

"Voice! Voice! Voice! Choice! Choice! Choice!"

Then she told me this little story about how she invented a method of transcendence over negatives. She added an important note: that when a victim takes control, she is no longer a victim.

In Angelou's dictionary, transcendence is nothing more than a state of mind, an attitude. It works like an old-fashioned kaleidoscope. In the mysterious mirrors of her mind she rotated the bad things that had happened to her and, in the twisting of her imaginations, turned them into tools.

The first transcendence, dealing with child rape and its horrific aftermath to herself and the rapist, was the hardest because she was a little girl trying to find a way out of her own maze.

    ☙   I believe in endurance with grace. The person who endures and becomes bitter and callous remains hostile. But the person who endures and remains gracious despite traumas and pressures invites all of us to see how grand a human being can be. Writing helped me to open up to myself, to hold back nothing.

I was raped fifty-five years ago. Not one day has passed that I haven't thought about it.

After it happened, I fell into silence. I decided to think of my whole body as an ear. I said: "I'll eat all the sounds of voices, the sounds of words, the sounds of song, all the sounds." Silence can be good, in moderation. Silence is a way of dealing with things. People in various cultures meditate. Meditation is silence.

When I write, I'm not really in the room. I feel suspended. I'm in a different state. Maybe it's similar to the state people get into when they take hallucinogenic drugs. In a sense I do feel drugged. I feel "up," as in up off the floor by at least a foot and a half.

Self-pride is not just a tool. It's a condition. All virtues and all vices begin with the self. Without the pride of self, I could have no pride in anything or anyone. Self-pride is all embracing.

Before my son was born, I lived in an old car lot. I mean: I lived in an abandoned car. I found a nice car, got into it, locked the doors and fell asleep. I was awakened by fifteen kids. My neighbors. They also slept in cars. They helped me form my earliest ideas on multiculturalism.

The car lot became my house lot. My car was my house. I kept it clean.

During the day, if my father saw me on the street, he tipped his hat and kept on going. I had one of those fathers. My father had invited me to stay with him and his paramour. He was having affairs with everybody. His paramour tried to take her frustrations out on me.

She hit me. She stabbed me. Cut me.

My father took me to friends, not the hospital. He wouldn't have the scandal. His friends put Band-Aids on my wound.

When I woke up to what was happening, I walked out. I was afraid to go back to my mother. She had a temper. I was afraid that my mother would have declared war on my father. So I went back to the car life. When I healed, I went back to my mother. I said: "I want to come home."

Years passed.

When I was thirty years old, I went back to visit my mother. I had just showered and dried myself when she came into the bathroom.

She said: "Where did you get that scar?"

"That woman," I said.

"What woman?" she said.

And when I told her the story, she sat down and cried. Hysterical and angry she was. Full of temper. I knew that if she knew what had happened when it happened, she would have gone there and shot "that woman." I saw my mother then ... and then I knew. I knew! I had done the right thing.

I like myself for trying to be a good human being. Sometimes I blow it. But goodness is my intention. I like that quality about myself.

I'm a truth seeker. Human beings change. Truths don't change. The truth is immutable. Like the air, it is here.

I love the truth. There is peace and growth in truth.

Maybe that sounds like a contradiction. It isn't. Growth pertains to the turning of the soil. Peace, on the other hand, implies passivity. But there's a peace in growth because we were meant to grow. It's natural.

Nien Cheng

on courage

"What do you know of prisons?"

While Nien Cheng waited for my answer, she picked at a blueberry muffin, crumb by crumb. She held each crumb between her thumb and forefinger. She ate only one crumb at a time.

This is not how ordinary people savor a flavor.

During China's Cultural Revolution, during her incarceration in Shanghai's dreaded No. 1 Detention House, as she called it, Cheng was known only as Prisoner #1806. Cheng had forever conditioned herself to a severe regimen of self-rationing. Yet she had retained her sanity in the filthy cement cubicle that was her "home" for six and one-half years.

When fanatical agents had arrested Cheng ("Imperial Spy!"), she had been an executive with the Shell Oil Company in Shanghai, the widow of Kang-Chi Cheng, a diplomat. She was everything the merciless Communists despised: beautiful, pampered, prosperous, and educated in a foreign place, the London School of Economics.

Her jailers wanted to crush her indomitability. Break her spirit. Destroy her body.

She was tossed like garbage into solitary confinement. Police used violence to try to extract a false confession. She hemorrhaged. She was delirious. She had bouts with pneumonia. She was alone. She was in a "one-woman war."

It was beyond impossible to compare notes. Her experience was not my experience.

But I know a little about psychological warfare, about emotional abuse, about not being cowed by fences imposed by fanatics. I spoke to her of things I knew.

I told her that my war had been a much smaller war, that I had always wanted to rescue myself from an invisible jail of ignorance and to embark on an odyssey to be my best creative self. I told her I did not have either my father's blessing to study, or his monetary help.

When I was called "dumbbell," which was too often and for no reason, it was the same as being whipped. I never cried out in pain. But in the depths of my silence was born an implacable resolve to uphold myself. I told Cheng that I knew all about "one-woman wars," as my mother called them, and that I believe all wars are personal if you're fighting in one.

One ear cocked in my direction, Cheng absorbed all the nuances of me and my "prisons." A good interview involves making a connection and she had asked a fair question.

Why would Cheng care to share secret emotional truths about her torments in a Communist prison with a stranger—someone she'd never seen before and never would again? She wanted spoken proof that I, a journalist taking tea with her, understood something about being shackled, confined, reduced.

She then told me just how barbarous the barbarians were.

When her daughter, Meiping, a twenty-four-year-old actress in the Shanghai Film Studio, refused to "confess" that her mother was a spy, a Red guard—formerly an ordinary factory worker—beat beautiful Meiping to death.

She spoke eloquently and simply about the stuff of endurance.

The intense mother and daughter bond has always embraced and sustained me. I told her about my mother's stoicism and her beauty. Cheng bowed her head, ever so slightly, in a gesture of understanding and we met on common ground.

The worst time of the first year is the first month.

When I was first taken to prison, I thought of it as a unique experience. I said to myself: "Remember every detail." Do you think I'm crazy for being positive about something so horrible? Suddenly I was entering a place I had heard talked about only in hushed whispers. Suddenly I was there, a political prisoner of a totalitarian government.

You are locked in a small cell. You're at the mercy of merciless guards. You are cut off from the world. I was depressed. I was vulnerable. All I wanted to do was to get out. The guards threatened me. The psychological pressure was great. Freedom was implied. If I confessed, I would get out. I would not confess to a lie.

I was confused. But I had a goal: to clear myself of the charge that I was a spy.

I was not a spy. To be accused of spying was the ultimate insult. I wanted to clear myself. I felt I was fighting a personal war.

When I was being beaten, I could not fight back. There was no way for me to defend myself. Sometimes my arms were handcuffed behind me so tightly that my wrists bled. I was often kicked by guards who wore heavy boots. But I always kept my chin up. It was a simple childish defiance. I would have been beaten less if I didn't take that attitude. Even when I was slapped from the right to the left, from the left to the right, I kept my chin up.

When physical violence is actually being inflicted, you are numb with pain. I felt my body was breaking. For me, the room went round and round. I tried to recover my breath. I felt I was reduced to the level of an animal. The police tried to break my body but they never broke my spirit.

When I was interrogated, I pretended to be stupid. I wanted to irritate my interrogator, hit back a little bit. I'd say ignorant things that would incur some wrath. It was a kind of mind game. I found it intellectually stimulating.

The interrogations kept me alert, perked me up. Sometimes I was so hungry my stomach hurt. But I've always been able to think well on an empty stomach. I thought of the interrogators as a form of human companionship.

My cell was a dead place, a cement box in which I was entombed. The interrogations made me feel I was still alive. I never thought I was courageous. Courage is just holding on in a crucial moment. All of us are capable of courage. It's one of those hidden human resources. Courage is required only in moments. For me, those moments came during the interrogations.

I would rather die than lie. Simple as that. To lie is a sign of weakness. I was innocent. I was wrongly accused. I would not surrender the truth.

There were times I was taken in front of angry crowds who had been primed to revile me *en masse*. People spit on me. I survived these confrontations by telling myself that the crowds were ignorant, that they didn't understand.

I made a decision to rely on my sense of discipline. I don't make decisions lightly. I analyze the situation carefully. Once I make a decision, I don't turn back. No matter what. I see things to the precise finish.

Perhaps I'm not the type of person who would go crazy. I'm not an emotional creature. When my husband died, I didn't cry publicly. When the police came to our home and destroyed everything in it, the furniture and the art and the antique china and crystal, I didn't cry.

Some police in a totalitarian society ... use extreme cruelty to cover up their own insecurities. I was beaten by police like that, both men and women. These masochists enjoyed beating me. They were also beating their secret guilt. In my heart and in my mind, I felt I was right. That gave me the strength of endurance.

Chita Rivera

on attitude

Late one night in the dark, dangerous, superspeed labyrinth of big-city traffic, a taxi smashed into the car Chita Rivera was driving.

When she was rescued from a heap of shards of glass and twists of metal, it was obvious that one of her legs was crushed.

In the hospital, in the hazy distance that blurred a flurry of people in white uniforms working the machines that worked on her, she overheard something too terrible, too disastrous, something no dancer, no human, wants to hear. The people in white were whispering about Chita Rivera, dancer extraordinaire, becoming an amputee.

She wanted to scream "No!" but the unbearable pain erased her strength. In the corridors of her imagination she envisioned an angel. The angel was dancing. That's the last thing she remembers. The dancing angel.

In the operating room, they bypassed the saw.

Instead they used drills and twelve screws to hold the bones of her leg together. The doctors thought the prognosis was wonderful. They told her she'd walk again. Maybe. Dance again? They didn't think so.

Later, after she became a hit on Broadway again, when she danced her heart out, when she proved the doctors wrong, when she showed the world that hope and ambition are nature's natural Prozac, she spoke to me about being her own angel.

The angels may be up there, in the clouds. But when a woman is caught in a clinch, when she is stopped, she becomes her own angel. Every woman has an angel inside her. Rivera was, in effect, redefining the old adage that God helps her who helps herself. She simply gave it a feminine, and thus a feminist, twist.

How did Rivera mesh with the angel of herself?

She told me that the desire to dance again (she called it "a yearning impulse") was so strong, so overwhelming, that it became a force. She ordered the wounded part of her body, and her soul, to do what she wanted it to do. She equated this self-discipline with self-respect. She described stamina as nothing more than strictly-focused energy. She abandoned false pride. When she stumbled, when she fell, Rivera reached out to other angels, her caretakers.

Rivera believes that leaning on other people is not a sign of weakness but that you have to remember to return the favor. This is important.

The whole scenario, from crash victim to her physical and emotional victory over self, has become a credo of her self-empowerment.

She boiled it all down to one attitude: "To do rather than to think about doing."

When I had my bad accident, my doctor said facetiously: "You've done a great job on your leg." Then he said: "You're never going to get it all back, but you can go into therapy and see exactly what you've got left."

It never entered my mind that I'd never dance again. I can't explain my attitude to you except that dancers are taught just to get up and do. I put everything into "doing."

Yes, I got discouraged. Yes, I got depressed. Yes, I got impatient.

I stumbled! I fell! My faith was tested. But I also drew on my faith. I took the attitude: "Whatever I have left of the leg, I'll make the best of it." I also prayed that I could accept my attitude.

I had three therapists who were what I call my "silent angels." They never let me give up hope. Every time I took a step forward, I heard: "Good!" I grasped every positive word I heard.

These people, these angels, were put in my path to support me. They made me think I did it all myself. That's an angel. They never bragged that they helped me. This is what I mean by "silent angels."

The truth is that I've had to adjust to the limitations of my leg. My calf is still atrophied. I live with it.

I came into this world a dancing spirit. I have a dance impulse. It's a drive. It's a need. I have to dance. The impulse is what keeps me going.

The young hide behind the veneer of youth.

I am mature. Maturity brings you calmness. The love and passion you feel surfaces. The more open you are about yourself, the more deeply people react to you. It's as if you dare to let people know you as you are.

I had to learn to become a "presence." It took time. I met the challenge on stage, late in my career. During a play, in a moment of serious drama, the door to the set wouldn't open. I was supposed to walk through that door. I juggled the knob. Nothing happened.

I heard twittering.

I knew I'd lose the timing and the mood. Inside I was angry. But I calmly walked around the set and came to the place where I was supposed to be.

I looked out at the audience. They were aware of what happened. But I stood tall. I felt like I was the size of a mountain. My body language, my stance, told them not to laugh. Nobody did. There was not a sound.

That was how I learned to command. That's when I learned I could be a "presence."

I'm sorry I'm crying as I tell you all this. But I know you understand my feelings.

Emotions are part of the creative process. There's only one you. Only you have your feelings. I call on my emotions. I look for the truth in myself. When I trust the truth and translate it into the character I'm playing, I know I have tapped the real me.

I don't want just respect from my audience. I want heart. I want to be understood. I want to be loved.

Four times I was nominated for a Tony award! Four times! Each time I'd buy a new dress, go to the hall, the place loaded with gifted people, and wait. The moment of losing wasn't as bad as you might think. It was both a release and a relief. The anticipation of winning, the possibility, was finished. I understand finality. Losing is definite.

So is winning.

When I did win, I was wearing a black dress. It was not black for mourning. Yet, in recapitulation, I realize I was wearing black to honor the memory of my mother.

Then they called my name! I stood up! I felt like my mother. I thought she was there. All my life I felt I was dancing for her and for myself. At the moment of winning, I could feel her joy.

My mother had never said: "Win awards." She never told me to give up dancing and get a job. She just let me be me. We always knew, both of us, that I achieved everything for her.

When I won, I could feel her arms surround me like they had surrounded me when she was alive.

The mother-daughter relationship has always been important to me. When my daughter was born, I felt she was a gift. She was no longer in my tummy. She was in my arms, a being totally separate from me.

She reached up to me. Now I reach up to her. I share my emotions with her. We are friends the way my mother and I were friends. I also taught my daughter what I was taught: that discipline is based on self-respect. If you care about yourself, about how you look, about your reputation and about your talent—you're disciplined.

Stamina is something else. Stamina is focused energy. You

channel your energy. You don't waste it. If you use your stamina well, if you are disciplined about it, you enjoy your time on earth.

Time is very precious to me. There's so little time and so much to do. Living to be ninety is not the answer. What's important is making the time you've got count.

Jean Auel

on duty

The word *duty* figured big in my young life.

According to the father (not the heavenly one but the one at home), I had a duty that superseded all others: housework. There was no dish washing machine, except me. There were no prepared foods. The oven was moody. The washing machine had a wringer as opposed to automatic. Everything had to be ironed. My duty was akin to my mother's duty: wash-iron-cook-clean-wash-iron-cook-clean.

Whenever my father was out of earshot, my mother would always whisper: "Your duty is to yourself."

She let this sweet statement hang in the air between us like an exclamation point made of spun sugar. But I had a weekly award for my labor. When my father found me on my hands and knees scrubbing the kitchen linoleum every Saturday morning, he left me thirty-five cents: my grade school milk money, seven cents for each of the five school days.

I said: "Thank you."

He said: "It's your duty." The phrase was spoken as a commandment, and the authority that it represented was overwhelming. He wanted to break my spirit and, especially when I was crouched like Cinderella at work, sometimes he did. But deep inside, in a mysterious place which we call soul, a flame flickered and it kept alive the dream. I cannot explain how. I know only that the survival instinct isn't only physical.

My mother thought she couldn't escape what she called "our situation." I promised her that my escape would involve the two of us. Then we, co-conspirators, laughed because I always finished my promise with "It's my duty," which I pitched in my father's patronizing tones.

When I began to succeed in the world of journalism, I quashed my old memories of duty. I took the attitude that I had a duty to express my true self with words.

But I know what all women who are aware know: that forced duty is usually linked to rebellion. Rebellion isn't necessarily a bad thing. Success is usually rooted in rebellion gone right, rebellion that focuses channeled energy positively into a goal.

Then I met Jean Auel.

She brought up the issue of duty within the context of her husband's expectations of her duty as a housewife. Bells rang! She told me about being true to her own ambitions to be a writer when her husband insisted that her professional ambitions were alien to, and conflicted with, her marital obligations. His argument had a pivotal point: her duty to keeping the home fires burning.

Auel, who had written nothing before she turned forty, who had never gone to college, is the phenomenal author of four best-sellers all set in prehistoric times: *The Clan of the Cave Bear*, *The Valley of Horses*, *The Mammoth Hunters*, and *The Plains of Passage*. She was so good that her advances were in the $750,000 range. Her books have been translated into seven languages.

Against her husband's wishes, Auel, who had married at age eighteen and produced five children in six years, took an admissions test for a master's degree in business administration. Even without undergraduate credentials, she was a high scorer. Auel was forty years old when she received her MBA from the University of Portland.

While still in her fortieth year, she took another huge chance on herself. She quit her job as a credit manager of an electronics company in Portland, Oregon. She started writing stories longhand, on a yellow pad, in her kitchen.

Her husband told her she was being preposterous. They became antagonists.

She asked him: "Why do you want a stay-as-you-are-wife?"

He said: "That's what's expected of you." He was talking about duty.

When I first wanted to go back to school, my husband and I almost broke up. I felt constrained. I wanted intellectual stimulation. My husband wanted me to stay home, to take care of the children. He warned: "That's what's expected of you." Finally I said: "Look, I'm going to do these things."

I'm relating this to you with more ease than there was between us.

I think my husband felt threatened. He thought that if I was educated, I might find someone more interesting. He was insecure about me, not jealous. There were battles. He had to get over all cultural, societal notions. I had to believe I could do what I wanted to do. He had to believe I was capable of doing what I wanted to do and that it wouldn't interfere with our relationship. Now he feels real fine about my celebrity. He has a sense of respect for my intelligence.

The early feminists, particularly Betty Friedan, were catalytic. When I read Friedan, I felt I had permission to do what I wanted to do.

I grew up in the '50s. Friedan seemed to say to me: "You don't have to be fulfilled by motherhood alone. Don't feel guilty about fulfilling your desires." Then and there I decided to go to school. Friedan addressed problems that had no name, problems of feeling incomplete.

I had been asking myself: "Is there more?" I had asked myself: "Where's the rest?" There's something else I want you to understand. I never said to myself: "I want to write a book." What happened was that I found myself at a stage in life where I was bored with raising children, bored with the idea of working full-time, bored with my job.

My boss was twenty-six. I was forty. He felt threatened by me. I didn't respect him. So one day I just quit. That didn't make my husband very happy. Suddenly the family income was being cut in half. I had two children in college. I had to get another job. But I didn't even know what I wanted. Credit? Finance? Marketing? I didn't try very hard for a job. Oh, I sent out resumes. But I never sent one with a cover letter. What prospective employer is going to pay attention to a resume without a cover letter? Meanwhile I caught up with my sleep. I felt I was in some strong, floating space.

Late one night, I got an idea for a short story about prehistoric times. Mind you, just an idea. It was eleven o'clock at night. I remember it because my husband said: "It's eleven o'clock. Come to bed." I said: "Wait a minute. I've got an idea I need to try out." So I sat down at the kitchen table and started to write. It felt right. The characters just grew. But I was frustrated. I didn't know the details of my characters. What did they eat? What did they wear? What did they look like? Where did they live?

I really didn't know what I was writing, but a sense of curiosity overwhelmed me. It was just a little idea buried somewhere in my head. Next day I decided to consult Encyclopedia Britannica. I never thought that this scribbling was a new beginning. All I thought I was doing was filling up my time, playing around, before I got a real job. But step by step, I continued the writing journey. I went to the library. I consulted the catalogs. I went to the shelves and I found the books. I'd read, read, read. And I'd find myself saying: "Gee, I didn't know that."

If you dare to try your wings, if you start having small successes, that gives you the courage to go on. I was married at age eighteen. My mother wanted me to get married. It was expected of my generation. I had children, five in six years. I took care of them. I led a very ordinary life.

Now they're calling me a phenomenon. I don't think I'm a phenomenon. I've just gone though an evolutionary process. I was a successful mother. I was a success in business. I went back to school in adult life. I was a success at that. And then I decided to write and I became obsessed with writing. I never once considered whether or not I'd be published. I simply decided to do what I wanted to do. I wrote longhand on a yellow pad of paper. I started telling my story to myself. I got so caught up in writing that I resented the time it took for me to shower. In six months, I wrote 400,000 words.

But I haven't changed. At age forty, you've already lived a big portion of your life. Do you really want to know what this so-called phenomenon means to me? It means I don't have to go back to a corporate nine-to-five job.

I've also learned something else that's important. There's a big difference between being obsessed and being disciplined. Obsession is being pulled absolutely in a direction, to the exclusion of everyone and everything else. Obsession is saying "no" to everything but the obsession. Discipline is still wanting to write but allowing yourself time to stall. I can turn out some pretty fine meals. But the difference now is that I no longer resent the time I spend in the kitchen.

Carol Channing

on rejection

The message in every rejection is a variation on my father's "You cannot!" theme.

He meant that if there's a roadblock there, you don't have the stuff to get through it, past it, or around it. That was always how he cut me off.

Rejection doesn't hurt in one place. It hurts everywhere. The spirit to succeed is numbed. You think: "I know how to make the pain disappear. I'll abandon my ambitions."

It's hard to think of rejection as a passing storm.

When Carol Channing was eighteen years old, a producer fired her from her summer job. The dismissal had the taste of a spoonful of salt. The producer didn't blame it on a budget cutback. He didn't say that the part she played was being eliminated. He told Channing that her dismissal was based on his decision that she had no talent—none— and that she'd never amount to much.

Channing was well into her sixties when we talked about that moment in time. She was a living legend, a national treasure, a super-star. But that teenage rejection, delivered with an undertaker's cal-lousness, still stuck in her craw like the poison arrow that it was.

She spoke of the ramifications of rejection: that rejection makes it easy to succumb to paranoia, that rejection weakens you, that you begin to view the world as oppositional. Then she reduced rejection to its basic denominator. Rejection makes you doubt your abilities, the very talents that motivated you to put yourself out there in the first place.

The first firing made her suicidal.

Channing's soft-focus vision of death didn't match Jerry Lewis who, addicted to Percodan, told me he once put a loaded pistol in his mouth, fully intending to pull the trigger. Or Buckminster Fuller, the genius who invented the geodesic dome, who told me he'd gone to the shores of Lake Michigan, which he called his "drowning pit," to let the waters swallow him.

When Channing contemplated suicide, it was within the parameters of comedy. What she had in mind was a fantasy suicide. A temporary little death wish like, oh, maybe a car will run over me and that will be that. Her death wish was just a "mood."

Women are moody, I said, because they're sensitive and emotional. As my mother liked to remind me now and then, women have the God-given strength to withstand the pangs of birthing. That kind of fortitude spills onto every labor of love, including giving birth to a career. I told her I'd bet that she got over the suicide penchant pretty fast.

She giggled in agreement.

What was truly funny was that Channing was talking like a woman and she was dressed like a man.

Not just any man.

She was attired in a uniform like those worn by commanders of ocean-going vessels, including the appropriate shirt and tie and fancy braided cap.

It was obvious to me that her outfit was steeped in symbolism.

Surely Channing's fashion statement was designed to put across the idea that she had adopted the male philosophy that she, like any he, is the captain of her ship and the master of her fate.

Channing laughed uproariously. "Yes! Yes! Yes!" she said.

And then she told me this story.

When I was eighteen, I was fired by a summer resort producer. He said: "You should not set foot on stage. You have no talent."

I was suicidal with hurt.

I wish that I had said to him: "Stop treating me like scum!" But I headed home and I wished that a truck would drive over me. I thought: "People will think it's an accident, not suicide."

When I got home, my father was waiting for me with a letter. It was from the man who had fired me. My father tore the letter up in front of me. He threw it in the wastebasket in front of me. And he told me this: "That producer is crazy. He got satisfaction from firing you. That should have been enough. But he carried it further by wanting to hurt you in front of me. Don't listen to him. The letter proves he doesn't know what he's talking about."

I said: "Daddy, how can you stand by me?"

He didn't explain his attitude in words. He just stood by.

I didn't know it then, but I absorbed his encouragement by osmosis. I didn't feel supported. But I was overcome with one overriding thought: "If I don't make it, I'll die." So I kept going. I didn't leave a stone unturned. I thought: "Maybe they'll see what I see."

All this goes back to when I was eight. I was nominated for secretary of the student body in school. I had to go on stage, in the auditorium, to tell the students why they should vote for me.

I couldn't think of a reason. So I impersonated the principal. I impersonated my favorite teachers.

Suddenly I heard laughs. This was my first experience of communicating with an audience. I ran offstage, crying. I said to myself, excitedly: "This is better than affection." I said to myself: "We're all brothers and sisters. All people are basically the same." And it was all because they laughed at what I had laughed at. I was eight and already making up my mind to lay down my life to hear people laughing with me. I wanted more of the same.

I was only a child. But from that moment on, I didn't feel alone.

I'm a communicator. There's nothing noble about that. Communicating is sharing. Everybody wants to share. It has to do with the desire to be part of the human connection. My father died twenty-five years ago. He is still the deity of my life. One of the last things he said to me before he died was: "Happy people are working people who use every sinew of their body to be the best at what they do." He said: "The people who try to escape work are unhappy, miserable."

When I work, I use all my intelligence. When I'm not working, I don't feel normal. When I don't work, I don't perceive life as being a tremendous experience. When I don't work, I don't believe in anything—except the belief that I'll work again soon. When I work, I'm not aware that it's work. It just seems right.

I don't equate work with endurance. It has to do with commitment.

Alice Walker

on heroines

One of the most fascinating aspects of Alice Walker's personality is her pervasive aura of tranquility.

Perhaps it is rooted in the fact that she has grappled with demons, survived and, in the process, has found her own powerful voice. No one tells tales of victory better than Walker.

She is someone who ignores the extraneous to concentrate on the essential. Reducing everything to its common denominator is reflected in Walker's no-frills style of dressing: a black T-shirt that melts into black pants.

The personal drama of Walker, whose 1982 novel *The Color Purple* won a Pulitzer Prize and was made into a Steven Spielberg movie, erupts like a volcano when she speaks. Her voice is mellifluous, but the word pictures she paints release a powerful blast of emotions.

When Alice Walker was eight years old, one of her brothers aimed a BB gun at her face and pulled the trigger.

Her right eye was permanently blinded.

When she was fourteen, she underwent surgery to remove what she described as "a glob of whitish scar tissue" from the eye.

But it remained sightless.

The shocking thing about this, beyond the fact that she has only one eye that works, is that she helped to spin a cover-up story that placed no blame or responsibility on her brother.

When Walker told me this, I asked: "Why? Why? Why?"

Why, in effect, did she shield her brother?

Why did she, a blinded little girl, lie to protect her brother?

Her self-imposed silence, which she explains simply, is infinitely more complex than it appears. I have only a snippet of her truth. But the snippet is something Everywoman who has ever been hit with the myth that males have a birthright of superiority will understand.

She told me she kept the truth a secret to get her brother off the hook in terms of punishment, guilt, and remorse. As a half-blind little girl, she succumbed to the theory that males were born with a higher rank of authority and value. That was her gospel. She thought that her femaleness made the situation acceptable and therefore something to be endured.

That's why she lied.

Walker also thought it was heroic to carry alone the burden of what really happened to her eye. She called it duty. But it nearly drove her mad. There is never peace when you are stuck in the yoke of human bondage.

Her family were poor sharecroppers in Eatonton, Georgia.

Her father never made more than $300 a year.

Her mother worked as a maid for $17 a week. By the time she was nine, blind in one eye and keeping the "how" of her blindness locked inside herself, she accepted her other duty: to clean the house and cook the meals.

This is the same Alice Walker who is a graduate of Sarah Lawrence College. This is the same Alice Walker who received a Radcliffe College Alumnae Association Medal for her contributions to the community of women. This is the same Alice Walker who wrote *Possessing The Secret of Joy*, an indictment of the mutilation known as female circumcision, the removal of the clitoris, usually by a male family member at home and with no medication.

She champions suppressed women because she despises suppression in any form.

Walker doesn't say a lot.

She says a lot in a few words.

My brother shot me. I hated him then but, still, I tried to protect him. I claimed he hadn't done it. We had made up a story, that I stepped on a wire and it snapped and hit me in the eye. I did this knowing full well that my brother had aimed the gun and shot me.

Later I realized that my parents had bought the gun for my brothers. The purchase was directly related to the cowboy movies the boys saw on Saturday night. Early on, the boys were taught that men had guns and used them.

At the time, I was fearful and depressed. But I was happy when I realized that I wouldn't be totally blind. It was a struggle to carry on with just one eye. All the reading I've done has been with half the vision that I had. But this experience has connected me to people who have disabilities.

As a child, I had to be heroic beyond my capacity. I cooked and cleaned for people who weren't particularly appreciative. I also worked in the fields.

Now, looking back, I can see that it was an intolerable situation for everyone. But then I was suicidal. I thought about jumping off the roof of the barn. I didn't know the word "oppressed." But certainly I knew the feelings of oppression.

We had terrible housing in the middle of nowhere. But it was smack in the middle of the countryside. I bonded with the earth, with the spirit of nature.

I walked miles and miles through the forest and beside streams. I felt accepted by nature. I saw myself as an earthling. And that gave me peace.

I'm always in my dreams. It's like having another life. Sometimes my dreams are enigmatic. But there's always a truthfulness to them. Dreaming is a way to contact your subconscious in a way you can't access by any other method.

When I awaken from a dream, I try to remember how I felt.

If I am left with anxiety, I know that whatever the subject of my dream was, needs to be explored.

Sometimes self-scrutiny is painful. But I know that just behind the door liberation waits.

If I awake with a feeling of bliss, I know the problem is settled.

Writing is a form of prayer. It's a way to explore your deepest selves. And I do mean selves. I've made the acquaintance of my many selves. The selves have to be knitted together. It's what makes a person whole. When you absorb all your selves, you affirm yourself. You become weller and weller.

Motherhood is a hidden miracle. Every human on the face of the earth came from a womb. Every ordinary little woman scurrying along has probably given birth.

Women are heroes.

Shelley Winters

on independence

Shelley Winters would not please Miss Manners. She is an ode to independence, let the chips fall where they may. I learned the specifics of her sense of independence firsthand.

Each one of my interviews was preceded by a game designed to avoid the interview or, at least, delay it. This is a woman who thinks of an interview as a form of time tyranny. She is tied to a schedule. She does not like to be tied to a schedule. She played the interview game her way.

Our first interview almost didn't happen. The timing was perfect. She stepped onto a down elevator at the exact moment I was stepping off the adjacent up elevator. I was on my way to interview her in her suite. She was in the process of escape.

As the door of her elevator slid to a close, I overheard her say to the elevator operator: "Take me to the jewelry store on the first floor. I want to shop." She had left word with the maid to let me wait in her suite. I waited and waited and waited. I waited over an hour.

When she returned she found me sitting on a couch in the hallway to her suite waiting, waiting, waiting. "Hey," she said, "lemme show ya!" And she pulled out her purchases: a wonderful gold chain and a thick bracelet to match. She was wearing a new watch. She was funny and honest and we talked. Not a word of independence was spoken. Actions speak louder than words.

The second interview, in New York, was a half-day late. Apparently she had a serious row with her daughter about the use of a limousine for which Winters was to be billed. Winters had said "no, no, no!" because she didn't know any of the people who'd be using it. Independence has a price. Winters's publicist advised that Winters was in a "state" and had to have an emergency session with her psychiatrist before she could see me. When we finally met, in a hotel restaurant, Winters ordered a double martini. Not a word of independence was spoken. It was obvious that the Shelley Winters brand of independence had put her in an emotional straitjacket. I didn't print any of the things she told me about her fights with her daughter.

The third time, she wanted me to see her latest movie and she suggested to her manager that he get me two press passes. He laughed in her face.

"Cheapskate! Cheapskate! Cheapskate!" she screamed back. Then she stuck out her tongue. When he pretended he heard nothing, she slapped him the face with two words: "Fucking asshole!" She even offered to take me to the movies herself. What a fool I was to honor a looming deadline instead. What fun it would have been to go to a Shelley Winters movie with Shelley Winters.

My best and last interview with Winters was much shorter and much more to the point. It was as if she remembered all the actions, the plays, that preceded this talk and, finally, she spoke of her independence and called it by its rightful names: a blessing and a curse.

There is a great intimacy to one-on-one interviews. You are face to face with another person who is answering personal questions that are usually voiced in a psychiatrist's office. Shelley Winters turned the tables on me. She asked me what I thought about independence. Was it a good thing or a bad thing?

I said it was not an easy thing.

Shelley, I said, when you break away from the crowd, when you rail against ordinary everyday restrictions, you can find yourself alone. Sometimes it's nice not to answer to anyone. You can be self-indulgent and not explain yourself. But sometimes that kind of aloneness prevents you from matching feelings and experiences with other people.

That's isolating. What is life without direct, uncomplicated communication?

This was her answer.

🐛 I'm emotional. Emotion makes an actor interesting. The writer writes. The actor feels from his or her repertory of feelings. It's called effective memory. You dip into things that have happened to you, things past.

When a script requires sadness, I remember my mother's funeral. Or the time I thought about committing suicide.

Positive memories can also be a powerful tool. I remember riding next to my father in his blue Essex. I was dressed in a pongee dress my mother had made for me. I was happy. Or the first time I held my baby in my arms. Or the first time I got an Oscar.

For most people, life is generally blurred. That's good for most people. Nature has provided memory blocks. The bad things that happen are put away. The good things fade. But, to an actor, drawing on these emotions is a valuable tool. I don't always keep my cool. It's not easy to confront your emotions. I can go bananas. After a difficult scene, I need a half-hour of absolute quiet.

I wish I wasn't fat. Being fat is painful. My real friends like me if I'm fat or thin. Every so often, I give up cigarettes and booze. I go on a diet. Last year I lost fifty pounds. I've gained back fifty-one.

One of life's pleasures is wonderful food. I know I'm associated with a forkful of food in my mouth. A long time ago, Ingrid Bergman told me that, after thirty, a woman can have a pretty face or a pretty rear end. I told her I'd think it over and make a decision. You can see my decision, right?

I've lied to myself. A typical lie is: "I don't care if I'm fat or thin." Or: "I'll get the job because they'll recognize my talent." It's a lie. I'm smart enough to know that. Lies never work. No matter how stinky or lousy reality is, don't lie. I'm still lying to myself about being fat.

There are some things I don't lie about. I've read that I'm temperamental. If I think something is right, I'll fight for it. I've fought with the captains of ships. I like to fight with intelligent people. Someone insecure gets rigid in an argument. Some fights I win. Some fights I lose. And, of course, you have to know when to back off.

Hollywood is an unreal world. Most people are in it for the money. They do second, third, and fourth imitations of their first commercial success.

I'm an independent woman. I always want to close the door and know I'm in my own space. Independence is very important to me. Who says you have to sleep eight hours, get up and have breakfast? Sometimes I get up at 3:00 a.m. and have breakfast.

I don't want to change my lifestyle, my habits. I want to work when I want to work. I want to sleep when I want to sleep. I want to walk around naked when I want to. Marriage requires too much accommodation. Which may explain why I've had three husbands. In the true sense, independence is the privilege of doing what you what without considering another person. My independence spills over to my career. I want roles that make a statement about the human condition. I can't always find them.

All theater should elucidate. It should be an armory against despair and darkness. I see greed everywhere. Greed is a disease like tuberculosis is a disease. We need an antidote. Greed, in all its forms, has to be exposed.

What happens on stage and in the movies is the vanguard of the values of our times. Sometimes our values stink. You want to know what I really want? I want to make a difference in the ascent of man.

See, I've made mistakes. I made a considered decision to be a blond screwball. I played the parts. But I also did a lot of pictures where I portrayed women as victims. Maybe I helped to fertilize the ground known as the feminist movement.

I've been in therapy a long time. It has taken time to understand what my life's experiences have taught me. My therapist is a friend with whom I talk in an isolated circumstance. That's what therapy is: talking. Let me tell you one more thing about therapy. I want to understand the patterns of me. One of the things I have always wanted is self-esteem. Self-esteem is making a decision on the basis that you know what you know. Do I have self-esteem finally? Ha! That's the $64,000 question.

Sometimes I do. Sometimes I don't.

Agnes DeMille

on never relinquishing
the possibilities

Agnes DeMille, one of the greatest choreographers of our century, limped into her Greenwich Village apartment. It was a shabby place, dusty, the furniture worn and the room cramped. DeMille was gnarled and leaning on a cane and she had the perpetual look of someone whose rage had not yet worn itself out. She was seventy-five then and paralyzed on her right side. A massive stroke had consumed one-half of her once-agile body. She was on a new quest: learning to write with her left hand.

She didn't say hello. She quoted John Lennon: "Life is what happens to you when you're making other plans," she said, with difficulty, and she swung her cane in the air, twirling it in the general direction of a seat, her way of saying: "Sit down!" I was going to help her to a seat and, reading my mind, she snapped: "God helps those who help themselves." She sunk onto a couch. Half of her body didn't cooperate. She looked like a human pretzel.

"They used to call me a tyrant," she snapped. "Now I'm a cripple."

It took fifteen years of professional struggle in the world of dance for Agnes DeMille to be an overnight success. In 1943, when she choreographed *Oklahoma!* in a style so breathtakingly original, she got star recognition, critical raves and the kind of ratification that made her a dance deity. She went on to choreograph *Brigadoon*, *Carousel*, *Paint Your Wagon*, *Gentleman Prefer Blondes*, and *Rodeo*.

Her enormous success, coupled with the years she spent in analysis, didn't erase the memory of two words her uncle, movie producer Cecil B. DeMille, spit in her face: "You're ugly!" She still spoke of it. Also unerased was the memory of her equally-caustic father, William, a playwright, who scorned her. She still spoke of that too.

It was a sunny afternoon. Nature's bright lights streamed through the dirty windows and enveloped her in a dusty glow. There was something oddly amusing about what she wore. Red pants topped by a tunic that was printed like a newspaper. When I told her she had picked an appropriate fashion, she laughed and said she wanted me to print a story about making the best of bad times.

She told me that she still went shopping and that the grocer tied her packages to her wrist. She told me that elderly people in her position avoid taking baths and that the one thing she'd never stint on is paying someone to help her bathe daily. She said that when she's alone and tried to get around, she crashes into things but "little things like that" wouldn't make her stop trying to get around the apartment.

I asked her to tell me what she valued most of all in her condition?

She said that what she held dearest was her voice. "I don't know what I would have done if I'd lost my speech." And on that afternoon, as the shadows lengthened and she became very tired, we talked about her many trials. And the last thing she said to me, the thing that I'll always remember is: "Never give up. Never. Show them that ugly can be beautiful."

~ When I had my stroke, it never occurred to me that it was unjust. Injustice was not the situation. It was a physical problem. I had broken a physical law. I never rested. I pushed myself. I strained, worried, grieved.

I was ambitious to the point of being insane. I knew I had high blood pressure and that I wasn't careful. I took pills. But not absolutely, regularly. Suddenly, suddenly, an artery burst in my head.

I felt nothing. I don't know when the stroke occurred. No dizziness. No pain. The blood had diffused through the brain before the stroke took over. Then, then it started. Oh, brother! In two hours I was in the hospital. I was babbling. I was drooling. I made sounds that didn't make sense. I was beginning to forget. I was getting drowsy. I remember the ambulance. My arm dropped off the side of the stretcher. My arm never moved again after that.

I didn't know my husband loved me as much as he did. Married people, you know, get very used to each other, take each other for granted, and you wonder: "Is there any love left?" Well, love is love. It's something you can see. He brought me back. My husband loved me back into life. It was like bringing a dead plant back.

The nurse, the great one I had in the hospital, said the noblest organ in the body, my brain, had received the greatest insult. I was going to call my book, *Insult*. But the word didn't take in my recovery, adjustment, this whole reappraisal of my life.

Oh, I have regrets. My biggest one? I wish I could have done better. There are better choreographers. But when I got ill, I stopped hitting my head against a wall because I was not like somebody else. I reconciled myself to my life. I have people I love around me. And I'm still pretty arrogant.

The struggle never gets easier for a dancer. I was refused by every Broadway show before 1943. I'm not one of the gang. Never have been. That was always the trouble. A woman has to be seductive, flirty, lovely, clever. I was busy, harassed, not attractive. Attractive means time and energy and I didn't give attractiveness time. I was told that I had no sex appeal. But when I got on stage, I got yells of laughter. And I could make an audience cry.

What saved me was my stubbornness, pure stubbornness. I get stuck in ruts. I made up my mind to do something and I do it—whether it gives me pleasure or not.

I really don't have much physical courage, but I have courage in situations that demand moral conviction. If it's right, if it's proper, I don't think of the consequences. I don't hesitate. I say: "This is goddamn unfair!" That means I am alone. But I don't mind being alone.

I've not had a test, a real test. There is a certain courage of duration, courage not to whine, not to complain.

When I got to be a director, the rivalry was so intense, it was shocking. Women directors have a filthy time on Broadway. A woman cannot experiment. She has to be right or she is replaced immediately. And all theater is experimental. I always worked with closed doors. There were rivals who wanted to witness the ingredients of my first big success, *Oklahoma!* I threw them out of rehearsal, all of them. To the real Philistines, I said: "Get out! I cannot think with anyone as powerful as you around. Leave me alone! It's not possible for you to be wallpaper."

Yes, yes, I was called "difficult."

I don't know what to think about reincarnation. There was only one Shakespeare. There's never been another. Possibly there will be another me, but I doubt it.

Helen Hayes

on beauty

It was a riveting moment and it held me in its stranglehold. Helen Hayes, a handsome woman of enormous strength and resourcefulness, someone who'd never consider unfulfillment an option, was admitting the unthinkable: that she didn't think she was then, or ever had been, physically attractive. Who'd ever have thought Helen Hayes had low self-esteem?

In truth, she was gorgeous.

What streamlined her handsomeness were the renderings of her heart. She had an inner light. That is the greatest beauty of all. But being on the stage, in the movies, on television, she was constantly compared to tall stringbeans whose faces translated into perfect symmetry when the lens and the lights were right. Helen thought that, in comparison, she never measured up.

She was eighty-nine years old when she made this confession. I've always believed that the most important thing she said to me that day was this: the best thing a woman can do is turn a deaf ear to anyone who mentions any physical imperfections. Helen said that Greta Garbo, who was Perfection personified, never listened to prattle about her looks. "You know," Helen said, "when I first started in the movies, I was told I only had half a face. I was told by the cameramen to be photographed only from my right side. It was as though only half my face was reasonable. It was demeaning."

She had invited me to her 21-room Victorian house in Nyack, New York. We sat together on the veranda, with its spectacular view of the Hudson River, and she served iced tea, punctuated by fresh sprigs of spearmint, in crystal goblets. She wore a blue silk shift dress. Her white crown was coiffed to perfection. Her pink lips matched her manicure. She was old, but her beauty was classic.

When she tired of the veranda, we went into a sitting room with curved love seats and romantic fainting couches and, in the midst of the decorative splendor that looked like a stage set, she spoke of her inferiority complex.

"In my youth," she said, "I had a pretty average-looking face and form. I had no special attributes." Before I had a chance to contradict her, to remind her that her present prettiness was a continuation of her past prettiness, she spoke her mind. "Now, when I get gussied up with paint and powder, they say I'm exceptional." I wanted to tell her how exceptional she really looked. But she stopped me again. "I look less than an eighty-nine-year-old is supposed to look."

She told me that her husband was witty and that he was drawn to her because she appreciated his wit. There was no talk about her beauty. She told me that she had spent years working to improve her posture and her carriage because she wasn't beautiful—and these were compensations. She told me that when she had fits of wanting to appear beautiful, she went out and bought fancy clothes and ended up hating them—and herself—for falling for what she termed elaboration.

How did she finally come to terms with the issue of non-prettiness? How did she effect some closure? She developed this credo. It always worked. Whenever she was beset by feelings of self-doubt, she chanted to herself: "I have no desire to be noticed. I've already had notices."

Her redeeming mindset was, simply, that if she judged herself by the beauty of her work she felt beautiful. And that's how I learned that the great, the magnificent Helen Hayes measured her beauty in terms of two Tonys, two Oscars, an Emmy, and a Grammy.

〜 I'm super-critical of myself. When I see myself on tape or film, I think things went wrong. I think: "If only they'd given me another chance, I could have done better."

When I first started in the movies, I was told by the cameramen to be photographed only from my right side. I was overwhelmed by the limitation. Too bad. I should have been like Greta Garbo. She never listened to prattle.

My mother trotted me to hotel lobbies in Washington and New York to see The Swells. I wasn't impressed with The Swells. I had no wish to waste my time, or my imagination, trying to be A Swell. I had other roles in mind! The Swells didn't awaken in me the desire of imitation. Ah, if I knew then that I'd play a Queen, I would have watched how The Swells walked. They walked like queens.

Anything I've attempted to learn was to better myself as an actress. I had to increase my understanding of people. I became a people-watcher. Actually I became a great starer. I made up stories about the people I stared at. I wrote their biographies. That's how I studied character. In a university, you are given assignments. I gave myself an assignment: know yourself and the world around you and the people in it.

I never wanted to be known as "cute." Cute is making a conscious effort, tricks, to make people think well of you. I never used tricks. But I've been accused of being cute and tricky. I've always resented that. I've decided, finally, that I've been called "cute" because I'm small. Small is cute.

I spent years studying ways to improve my posture and my carriage. Ah, that's my secret. I startle people because I stand straight, sit straight, and walk straight. I don't have a hump in my back. So now people say: "Why, you're beautiful!" They don't know my little secret. I just say "Thank you."

When bad things happen to me, I don't give in, cry, yell, faint, or scream. I stand back. I look inside me. Actually, when bad things happen, like losing my daughter and losing my husband, I get a bad cold.

When my daughter died, she was nineteen.

I was in the agony of severe anxiety. I tried to go for walks, but people on the street recognized me.

First their faces lit up in recognition and then their faces fell. I am a performer. My presence is supposed to give people pleasure. But I didn't give anyone pleasure.

So I fled to a friend's ranch. I kept out of sight. My bad cold got worse. It was a deathly cold. I stayed in bed. I was incapacitated. I didn't move. I was engulfed in silence.

The silence helped me recuperate. Silence is healing. Silence releases the mind from upheaval, confusion and pain. When bad things happen, I lie still. I don't stir. I think of better days to come.

When I first met my husband, I thought he was utterly charming and witty. We laughed together and our laughter was a bridge to a quick friendship. I appreciated his wit and he appreciated me for appreciating his wit.

He drove me home that night and I knew I was in love. It wasn't his sexiness. It was, simply, that he talked good. He wasn't pompous. But he came out with the right words. He wasn't jealous of my success. He wanted me to be as well-known as I am.

But he was a proud Scotsman. He didn't want to be known as Helen Hayes' husband. When he felt he was sliding into anonymity, his pride was hurt. But he never tried to get into the act. The marriage wasn't perfect. It was perfect enough.

My husband's only weakness, alcoholism, made me feel I had to get away from him sometimes. I thought maybe I'd failed him. The alcoholism gave us terrible anxieties, terrible scenes. I didn't leave him alone about his alcoholism. Maybe I should have. But there wasn't any bitterness. My husband had grace. To have grace is to do things in the least hurtful way or, on the other hand of the spectrum, in the most delightful way.

Vikki LaMotta

on being battered

Helen Hayes didn't think she was pretty. Vikki LaMotta knew she was long on prettiness. Long wavy hair. Long nails. Long lashes. Long legs. Long glances. Besides, the sum total of her beauty seemed to be intact a long time. When Vikki was a fifty-seven-year-old grandmother, she posed nude for a *Playboy* centerfold. Reportedly, it was unnecessary to touch up the photographs.

Vikki was familiar with the argument that her *Playboy* peccadillo was perceived, by some, to be an ego problem.

She begged to differ. She had an ulterior motive. But it had nothing to do with being a show-off.

Vikki said *Playboy* was her way of showing the world that "society needed to see a woman who cares about how she looks ... a woman who has had problems, big problems, and lived—and looks like this because she didn't get bitter."

Vikki LaMotta is the second wife of Jake LaMotta, the 1949 middleweight champion who lost his title to Sugar Ray Robinson. The film *Raging Bull*, which stars Robert DeNiro as Jake and Cathy Moriarty as Vikki, is the story of a fading boxing star who could not cope with defeat or liquor, who went on drunken rampages.

But no one plays Vikki the way Vikki plays Vikki because Vikki, in person, is brutally honest about being a battered wife. No movie script can tell it the way she does in person: from the dark side of her memory machine, from the terrible "why?" of being boxed by the boxer. After the beatings, she didn't look good. When she healed, she didn't feel good inside. She felt aggrieved and anguished. Vikki believes that the kind of bitterness that assaulted her soul works faster than time to age a woman. His brutishness killed their love.

When Jake beat Vikki, she hated him as passionately as she had when she loved him. His blows numbed her into senselessness. Her fear was so intense that it stifled her natural power to scream. She stiffened into a real life punching bag. What had nudged the bull into a rage was Vikki's daring to articulate an opinion, a point of view, that was contrary, or even different, from his.

The raging bull expected his wife, the mother of his three children, to be a "yes" wife. He equated "yes" with marital obedience. Occasionally she was, in Jake's eyes, unpredictable. Her expected "yes" was replaced with an occasional "maybe," or a "perhaps" or, the worst, an "I think." Vikki was expected to be opinionless and subservient. She even arrived at the point that whenever an original idea or a reaction popped into her brain, it was accompanied by a flashing red light that snapped one word into her consciousness. "Prevent! Prevent!"

But a woman can't always and forever squelch her voice. The more Vikki strove to be heard, the more violence she encountered. Jake was convicted for attempted burglary and sent to prison. They were divorced in 1958, after Jake's release. He lived in New York. She went to Miami. Long distance helped the healing. She spoke her mind to him on the telephone.

All the questions I asked Vikki, a battered wife who brought her daughter Christi along to hear her story firsthand, centered around one question with two sides.

Where did the bitterness go? How did she manage to flush it away?

Christi listened and cried quietly. Vikki did not cry. I've never liked having my interviews audited. But, in the end, I was glad Christi was there. What Vikki had to say was an ode to her daughter, to all daughters who have seen their mothers physically abused by their fathers. Christi had seen and heard much. But this time, through the catalyst known as the interview, her mother put all the jagged pieces of the family puzzle together in one terrible swoop. The picture the pretty woman painted was not pretty.

∾ I was sixteen years old when I met Jake LaMotta. He was twenty-four. A boxer. He worked out in a gym near where my father, a butcher, worked. I was a freshman, James Monroe High School. The South Bronx. You know, in those days, a girl didn't talk about careers. A girl talked about who she would marry and when. The talk was always about the man of your dreams. Talk about a career? Never!

The neighborhood I grew up in, it was tough. The boys, they were aggressive. Sexually and otherwise. And I was extremely attractive. Outstanding compared to the other girls in the neighborhood. It got so I was afraid to walk down the street at night. Or to get in a car with any of them. Then I met Jake LaMotta. It was at a neighborhood pool. I loved him right away. I loved his face. His eyes. He was gentle. Very low-key. Very tender. The men in the neighborhood were rough. Rough and tough. Jake showed me a beautiful love. I felt protected. So we got married.

My parents never sat me down to discuss things. They never said: "Why are you doing this?" or "Don't do it." There was no conversation about getting married. My family life was beautiful. In the beginning, I loved his mother, Elizabeth. And his father. Jake LaMotta adored his children. And I was forever good, the obedient girl. I loved being pregnant. I loved nursing my children. I had three. And everything was beautiful because I served him. Served! And listened. I was obedient. Obedient! You see, I subjugated myself. I never allowed my feelings to surface. I was a child bride. I acted like a child. Waiting to be told, being submissive and docile. I had not yet matured.

When you're obedient (and I was an obedient child), you are rewarded. Everyone likes you. You don't get spanked. I didn't realize, until later, that they like you because you're doing what they want. I was ignorant. Good but ignorant. Then I learned to say: "Hey, wait a minute." And that's when the conflicts started. He, Jake LaMotta, champion, was used to obedience.

Did I talk to him about his feelings, his failures? Talk? Oh, I wish we had. There was no input from me. I could have helped him. Could have influenced him. But there was this thing about a man listening to a woman. I could never say: "Hey, Jake, I think ..." I was not supposed to think. I was supposed to be obedient. I knew Jake couldn't handle a drink ... and once he started to drink, he drank more. And the more he drank, he became violent. He beat me, yes, he beat me ...

It took a long time to find myself as a person.

The real, real trouble started when Jake was nearly thirty. He had been told that a fighter who's thirty years old is all washed up. He had this psychological fear that he could not continue. That was a part of it, the idea of losing his grip on the only trade he knew. Boxing.

The other part was that Jake LaMotta was no longer on the streets. He had a beautiful home. He had a wife. He had his kids. What Jake didn't have was a desperate need to survive, to win. To train, you have to have extreme desire. That desire wasn't there. He wasn't deprived; he was the champion.

Then Jake started drinking. He was losing his ability as a fighter. He drank because life became increasingly difficult for him. What could he do to impress Vikki? He was in the ring to impress Vikki. And Vikki was not experienced enough to handle his fears.

At that time, psychoanalysis was not so open. What did I know of psychoanalysis? I knew Jake, who couldn't handle a drink, had a problem. I knew he needed help. And once he started to drink, he drank more. And the more he drank, he became violent. That was the beginning of the end, the violence.

The first time he beat me, my first reaction was: "This is dangerous." He beat me, yes, he beat me. The first thing I did was try to prevent the agitation. Prevent anything that would make him angry. But in the back of my mind, I wanted to leave him, to leave home. It was awful. I didn't want to be with this man. I wanted to be away from him.

When a woman encounters violence, a terrible fear sets in. It is a fear beyond sweating, beyond screaming. There is a kind of shock. You are so frightened, you freeze. So frightened that you don't feel your body. You don't feel anything because you're actually frozen. You want to grab a hold of someone. But there's no one there.

Look, no one told me anything. They just said: "Hey, you're beautiful, you don't need help." It's kind of like that with Jake. Jake's personality is not likable. He's abrupt. He's outspoken. He's not polite. No one is looking to help him. No one wants to help a champion.

I saw the play *The Miracle Worker*. Helen Keller couldn't find herself until she was beaten, dragged down, pulled across the floor. When that happened, she had a vision of herself. Jake, he needed psychiatric help, a hospital. Instead he was in prison. He hit the bottom. Like Keller. Much, much later we talked. I told him you've always got to answer for your actions in life. I told him: "You do something wrong, Jake, and there's no way you can walk away from it the same person." I told him: "The more you do ugly things, the more ugly you become."

This was the truth. He had to accept it. Jake LaMotta is not a happy man. He was never a happy man, not once in his whole life. His idea is that if you can get through a day or two without too much misery, that's happy ... I didn't talk to him like that when he was in prison. I had worries. I had to pay the plumber. To feed the kids. I couldn't deal with anything analytical. We talked later ... and Jake's attitude was good when I talked to him.

After prison, he moved to New York. It's easy to talk to

someone from a distance, from Miami where I live. He was miserable. I was not miserable. I had my children. That's what healed my bitterness. Am I to waste my life being bitter? I don't feel good being bitter? And I want to feel good. I'm not in pain. My children, they're not in pain. We have problems, yes, but our relationship is open and healthy. So why should I be bitter?

Dr. Joyce Brothers

on fear

My confession to succumbing to fear was not something I'd ever really talked about. But I was forced, in the nicest and most reasonable way, to articulate my fear of Fear in an interview with Dr. Joyce Brothers.

She always seemed so extraordinarily calm and cool, as if nothing could stop her, and I asked if she ever got scared, ever felt the pangs and panic of fear, and if she did, what was her coping mechanism?

I don't know why the question, which seemed fair, startled her. But it did. She heaved a heavy sigh. She looked at me hard, not with suspicion, but with genuine shock.

I realized instantly that material that I had considered innocuous had touched a nerve. It was as if the psychologist was being analyzed. Dr. Brothers was well aware that I was making a reputation for transforming newspaper interviews into bona fide conversations of exchanged ideas and experiences.

So she asked me to answer one question before she answered mine. Dr. Brothers wanted me to define fear, not according to the dictionary, but according to me.

I told her Franklin D. Roosevelt had it right: There's nothing to fear but fear itself. Fear is a sorry condition.

When fear snatches you, everything seems to stop. You can move, but you don't. You can talk, but your tongue is tied. You are paralyzed, frozen, and although you appear to be functioning normally, you are so scared that you feel sick and dizzy and nauseous.

Fear is a loathsome thing, worse than the worst migraine headache that is immune to the miracle of modern medicine. Fear is the chomping dragon lying in wait in the dark swamps of yourself, where the debris of bad experiences is filed but not forgotten.

Fear feeds on itself. To give in to fear is to give in.

I've known this for a long time. But I have not conquered the dragon. I've managed to hold it in abeyance, and only with occasional success. I look at fear and fear looks at me and it's clear that we each want to conquer the other. Fear wins more times than I do. I told Dr. Brothers that for me, fear (fear of rejection, fear of being misunderstood or misjudged, fear of giving my best efforts and seeing them fail, fear of being stopped by sickness, fear of losing the people I love) is the ever-present Fear specter.

When I was a little girl, I played a wonderful piano.

Sister Jeanne Rosa, my Catholic teacher who held her Protestant student dear, would proudly plan school recitals. My mother was excited: it was proof I was going to be a star! The idea of stardom excited me. I was seven years old and star meant Hollywood star and that meant pretty clothes, pretty people and the pretty sound of applause, of acceptance.

The reality of the being thrust onto a small stage, being put "on display," and the ever-present fear of striking the wrong chord and being harshly judged was a scenario that I squelched until my mother was driving me to the recital destination. When I saw the place of performance looming, I yelled: "Stop the car!" My mother knew what that meant. Fear had overcome me. I lunged out of the car and threw up in the gutter. I was a great Sunday School student then, the pianist for the children's choir, and I drew strength from familiar snippets like "I shall not want," "Fight the good fight," and "Onward, Christian soldier." Those thoughts were my crutches. They still are.

Then I rephrased my question to Dr. Brothers:

What are you afraid of?

⮐   I am afraid of everything. One of my worst fears, as a child, was having to sell Girl Scout cookies. The terror of ringing someone's bell. A stranger. I had a terrible fear of the door slamming in my face. I wanted to sell the cookies to my mother. She'd have none of that. What I feared most was rejection. A feeling of absolute terror gripped me.

I have been a guest on the Johnny Carson Show a dozen times. But there's a moment when I am gripped with fear. It's a moment before the curtain parts and I go on stage. My hands, they are freezing cold. I am panic-stricken. I think I'm going to make a fool of myself. And the Johnny Carson Show affords you the opportunity to make a panoramic fool of yourself. People are not fooled when a person falls flat on her face on national television. But once I get into things, I'm all right. It's that incredibly scary moment just before.

Fear is good sometimes. It is good to be scared that you will not do well. Fear forces you to do your best, to be your best. But it is bad to be so scared that you are paralyzed. Helen Hayes told me that just before she goes onstage, she is sick to her stomach. She feels physically nauseated. She is afraid, afraid. But courage is born of this nagging fear. Courage is the willingness to do something you're afraid to do, to do it well.

There is no fear in the idea of my own mortality. The great pain is loving the person who dies, the person whom you'll never see again. Never.

The alternative is not loving at all. People get so scared of being hurt, they freeze themselves. They don't get close to anybody. There is no warmth. That is my definition of hell, not loving. You can tell yourself that if you never go out of the house, you'll never be run over by an automobile. You can avoid being vulnerable, yes. But that's not living.

I'm courageous in my own way. I've faced criticism. As a so-called pop psychologist, I've reached a lot of people. Oh, I could eliminate all criticisms by never doing anything experimental. I like to try things, all kinds of things. Some work. Some don't work. If one thing out of ten works, I'm ahead of the game.

When I first started on television, psychologists did not deal directly with patients. The approach was the Freudian couch. Very classic. The doctor was a distance away. The doctor actually sat facing away. If the doctor raised an eyebrow or frowned or grimaced, the talking patient was unaware of the reactions. There was a safe distance between the doctor and the patient. Always, the patient was kept at arm's length, in a darkened room.

To me, that meant being kept in the dark, literally. I've changed that. I've always believed the informed patient is the better patient. I raised eyebrows. In 1956, I talked on radio about premature ejaculation. I said what caused it, what to do about it. At the end of the program, I looked up and saw a whole ring of male executives looking pale, panicked. They expected an avalanche of angry complaints. There weren't any. Only a lot of calls saying, "Gee, thanks, I didn't understand about that before."

Oh, sure, I felt twinges when I saw the executives' faces. Yes, yes, there was a moment of sheer panic. I asked myself: "What have I done?" But then the mail came and I was vindicated.

In the early '60s, I said homosexuality was not a mental illness. It was a very unpopular thing to say. Probably the most unpopular thing I've ever said. People would come up to me and say, "Homosexuals? They're sick, sick, sick." I got vituperative mail.

About the same time, I said that abortion should be an informed decision between a woman and her doctor. NBC-TV officials forced me to look at hours of film on fetuses being aborted. They said I must see the realistic side of abortion. But I have never changed my mind.

Yoko Ono

on prejudice

When Yoko Ono rocked The Beatles' all-male cathedral with the impact of her presence, she tasted the everlasting bitterness of gender prejudice. It haunts her still, long after John Lennon's murder and her widowhood. You can't read her eyes. Yoko hides behind dark glasses. You have to read her words. They echo the cry of Everywoman.

We didn't exchange war stories. But it is Yoko Ono's theory that the first step toward freedom from prejudice is to identify the prejudice. Air it. Confront it. I can tell you that's not an easy thing to do. But once done, if only within the lonely depths of your deepest self, is it possible to make some sort of peace with the unthinkable. Yoko did it. This is how I did it, imperfectly, knowing that the pieces of my soul will never fit quite the way they used to fit.

The land mine that exploded in my path was detonated by an impeccable male hierarchy: The Church, the real one, before females were bishops, ministers, acolytes, readers, vestry. The specific Episcopal Church I used to know was very macho.

It turned out that in the male bastion of that particular church, where my mother and I worshipped every Sunday, where she and I had sought solace and comfort together, I learned the hard way that I was regarded as an insignificant female, a daughter who had assumed the role of directing my mother's funeral exactly as she made me promise to do when we both knew that invisible monster, Cancer, started nibbling at her insides. The Church rejected me like The Beatles rejected Yoko. Their actions spoke louder than words.

After my mother died, and before her funeral, I had gone to the minister with the service my mother had mapped out—and which I had promised her that I would carry out exactly as she wished. She kissed me with her eyes when I promised, again and for the last time, what I had promised her countless times during her last year: that *she* had the last word.

Everything was firmly in place. Everything was going to be just as she had asked. My mother used to say that God was in the details. I had taken care of all the details.

The music in Yoko's life and the music I had chosen for my mother's funeral seem to have nothing in common. But the commonality is that she had some ideas about the Beatles' music and my mother, and I, had some ideas about the music for the funeral. Yoko and I hit an iceberg of enormous gender prejudice that made us outsiders in a world in which we thought we belonged.

The funeral service began. The majesty of organ music enveloped my mother's coffin, and me. But it wasn't the music I had chosen! I was sitting in the pew my mother and I had shared every Sunday for many years. Even in death's debilitating shock, when the intellect is numbed and the soul is weighted in unspeakable grief, I understood, again, that people are not created equal and that the chauvinism that I grappled with home had followed me into the inner sanctum of Church.

And my mother was a frozen statue in a box. She was never going to be at my side again. Never be my protector, my mentor, my applause. She could never say this was wrong, all wrong. The memory of that moment of that stark aloneness still leaves me limp. I know the emptiness Yoko spoke about, what she called "the incredible sorrow." And all the while the moments of my mother's funeral were slipping away, dying. There was no way I could make this right.

Then, to add shock to shock, I heard the minister, with whom I had made specific arrangements, read an Old Testament passage that he had said he liked and which I had specifically asked not to be read.

It was not a passage my mother requested.

What I had requested, in my mother's spirit, specific New Testament snippets, had been eliminated. Erased. Silenced. The Church also erased me. I could write a newspaper story. I could not write my mother's funeral and have it carried out as I had written it—exactly as she wanted it written.

The Church didn't warn me that it was going to whip its bitter chauvinistic bias on me, through me, around me. It simply made its position clear after the fact, when I was powerless to retort. It spelled out, again, what I'd always been told at home—and Yoko heard it too, in her life: that a woman cannot direct, that a woman is subservient to all men, even those who rule the altar, whatever that altar happens to be.

I have made a molehill out of that mountain by putting my prayers and faith in God within the sphere of my heart. I have eliminated the middleman, The Church. I pray, not in an ecclesiastical edifice, but wherever I am. I access life's benevolent Force by tapping into it myself. God helps her who helps herself. Yoko knows that.

    I'm just an ordinary person. I, too, have turbulent feelings. I experience sorrow and anger. But, at the same time, I'm always trying to transform negative feelings into positive feelings. I feel guilty when I feel hateful. I've experienced an incredible sorrow about what happened in December of 1980. It's easy to dwell on it. And I have. But that dwelling became destructive to my health. I knew I had to survive. So I started to work ... I'm a career woman, a workaholic.

When "it" happened, people told me to leave the Dakota. But I stayed in a place that for me was incredibly negative. I did a special project in Central Park [creating the "Strawberry Fields" sanctuary]. That project became my solace. Sometimes I just go there to watch people. They seem happy. Yes, they know who I am. People are very kind. They leave me alone.

In the beginning, when I first met John, I was naïve about the level of his fame. I didn't know what it entailed. John Lennon was a beautiful soul. He always gave me encouragement. Always. John left the Beatles in 1969, the year we were married. I was as surprised as anybody when he made his decision public.

All four Beatles simply "grew up." Each wanted to go in a different direction. They had done world tours. It became tiring. They had, in fact, become "the big show." Each of them felt they could not show their individual artistic ability. They were in a dilemma. They had become too big. John was constantly discussing this. The Beatles felt their music couldn't really be heard in concerts because there was too much screaming.

The Beatles were strong individuals. I'm a woman, a tiny one at that. The world gives me too much power. I've been accused of being the power that broke up the Beatles. It's just not true. Only the Beatles could break up the Beatles.

At first we didn't pay attention to the criticism of me. The prejudice against me was both racist and chauvinistic. I'm an Oriental, a woman who spoke her mind. No, I take that back. I didn't really speak my mind. But I sat next to John as an equal. The world was used to four Beatles, four men, sitting together and facing the world together. The ladies always stayed in the background. I challenged that stereotype. No, we challenged it together. That's what made it work. John was surprised at how willing he was to stand side by side with me.

John came from a macho background. Rock is macho. Guys in rock do what they want and they stick together. But he was in a partnership with the Beatles. He was practiced in the art of partnership. So, when we faced the world together, he was at ease with me as a partner.

The fact that his partner was a woman resulted in an incredible media attack. But that appealed to John's sense of fun. Smiling, he'd say: "Oh, they're upset, are they?" He saw the criticism as foolishness. He actually enjoyed the stupidity. It appealed to his natural sense of rebellion. John thought he was teaching the world a lesson. But he was surprised at the attack. However, that's how John came to understand what it meant to be a woman.

Coretta Scott King

on having "somebodiness"

It was a strange word, one that I'd never heard before, one that I never found in the dictionary. The word, "somebodiness," came from the personal vocabulary of Coretta Scott King, sitting like a queen, in the presidential office of the Center for Non-Violent Social Change in Atlanta.

"I believe in somebodiness," she announced, and the interview began.

We were sitting in her late husband's elegant office and, figuratively and literally, she was occupying his seat of great power and influence. None of this would have been possible, she said, without her being taught that grand old feeling of "somebodiness." She underlined that word with her voice, giving it additional impact.

In a way, Coretta Scott King didn't have to define "somebodiness." She embodied it. She exuded an air of unstoppability. At that moment, at least, there was nothing vulnerable about her. She was a warrior in women's clothing, a militant with a great manicure.

But I wanted her to break down the word "somebodiness," to detail it. I wanted to know how "somebodiness" works and, specifically, how it worked for her.

I told her that I, too, had always longed to be somebody, mostly because my father treated me like a nobody and, in my heart and mind, I carried around this invisible vision of myself as being professionally accomplished. That alone would make me "somebody" with a signature. We had a debate about the word.

Coretta said my vision of "somebodiness" (she still called it that) referred to an end result of success. She said her vision of somebodiness was about having an ongoing emotional arsenal of ammunition, building blocks, on which to forge an image and a career.

Weren't we talking about the same thing?

No, no, she said.

I was talking about an illusionary yearning, a dream that success would make me feel like a somebody. It should be the other way around. Success can be temporary. Feelings of confidence connected to that success can also be temporary. Coretta's concept is that real somebodiness is a state of mind with staying power. If somebodiness takes firm hold in childhood, you believe, truly and forever, that you are your own power. It's a permanent state of mind that has nothing to do with the comings and goings of success.

She said that if you had somebodiness inculcated into your mind frequently, especially by people whom you loved, you believed forever that you could do anything, be anything you wanted to be.

She knew that I knew that she was talking about the ideal. Wouldn't it be nice if somebodiness on that level became a female tradition, a requirement?

Coretta smiled. She asked if I had faced my life convinced of my own somebodiness?

I told her that I had manufactured my somebodiness as I went along, taking from each small success a smidgen of faith in myself and, in the long run of life, that had a cumulative effect on my self-esteem. Basically we were talking about the same thing: confidence. But we had walked different paths and our confidence had been tested in different ways. I asked Coretta if her sense of somebodiness had ever failed her?

She told me that her sense of somebodiness, a childhood gift from her parents, had an ironic twist. There were times when her "somebodiness" had been challenged and weakened. But, by the same token, her "somebodiness" had sustained her when life went bad. "With each strife conquered," she agreed, "you become stronger."

After all, she, too, had a dream, and it's still under construction. Somebodiness has to do with identity.

꙳ I was taught to have pride and dignity, to be an independent thinker. "Somebodiness" is letting nobody control you. It's not having anyone tell you how to think or what to do. There was financial insecurity in my family. But I was emotionally secure. I felt a richness of spirit and that made me feel rich.

I pondered myself, what I was created to be. I discovered my unique attributes. I never felt that I wanted to be anybody but myself. I wanted to be me. That's the essence of "somebodiness."

My father [a barber] taught me to be non-judgmental. He knew how people misuse each other but he was non-judgmental anyway. Martin was so much like my father. People liked to hang around my father and just talk. People liked to hang around Martin and just talk. My father had confidence and worked hard. My husband was like that, exactly. My father was never bitter. Martin wasn't bitter either. My father had an ego, you know, a typical male ego. But he never hurt anyone intentionally. That goes for Martin too.

At first, when I met Martin, I didn't understand the similarities. Subconsciously, what drew me to Martin was his warmth and aptitude for love. Martin embraced humankind love. He accepted people as they are. I knew that early in the courtship. People were attracted to Martin because, like my father, he saw their faults and loved them anyway. Martin would see drunks on the street, winos, who had lost their self respect. They wanted to touch him. They were reaching out for a Ph.D. who would not condemn them.

Yes, my faith has been tested.

When Martin was assassinated, I prayed for strength. I prayed that my strength could be transformed to those around me. Still, there were times I was weak, times that I wondered if I could withstand the pain. I've been physically exhausted too. But I've never stopped.

What sustains me is the belief, the sincere belief, that God has transforming powers. You can't blame God for all the bad things that happen. God is synonymous with good. I have taken that premise seriously. Individuals have to be creative forces for good. My life is a pilgrimage. But I grew into that pilgrimage. I didn't ask for it. But I've always wanted to do the right thing. The constant struggle, though, is this: to discover what is the right thing?

When I became Martin's wife, when Martin was no longer with me, what became important was that the direction of my life be in keeping with expressing my best self. People see me as an extension of Martin Luther King, Jr. I don't make decisions lightly. I weigh the impact of my actions. I've been accused of being indecisive. But I try to balance what's in my heart with my intellect. I don't always make decisions logically. When I do things I don't feel right about, they don't work out well.

Society has carved out roles for men and women. But that was never a barrier to my thinking. I've never seen myself as a person who would fit into the traditional female role. My parents instilled in me the idea that I had the intellectual capacity and physical strength to be the best, to achieve excellent in my life. I never felt limitations.

My parents were hard-working people. They were "deprived" in the sense they didn't have access to opportunities. But they convinced me of my personal worth, my somebodiness.

I'd like to see a more humane society, a more sharing society. I dream that we will resolve our conflicts without going to war with each other. My dream is not too different from the dream of anyone involved in human rights. I'm committed to the principles laid down by Martin. He dreamed of a society were there are no people are without a shelter, adequate food and enough income to sustain them.

Sometimes I think the struggle is impossible. I've seen nominal changes. I understand the foundation for human rights has been laid. The Center has come of age. When you're involved in a struggle and you don't see fast progress, you think you're going backwards. You're not. You're only standing still for a moment.

Tina Brown

on being an extrovert/introvert

When I went to the rarefied New York offices of Tina Brown, the world-famous editor of *Vanity Fair* and later the *New Yorker*, I did not expect the subject of "introvertedness" to take over the interview. Tina brought it up, placed it between us, dissected it. She has always liked to do the unexpected.

Tina Brown is a diminutive woman, small and compact. Her voice is a decibel above a whisper. Her clothes are deliberately plain: a Miss Marple tweed suit with a white shell. If Clint Eastwood was casting around for a librarian for an upcoming movie, she'd be the perfect choice. There's only one thing. She is a walking ad for the cliché that you can't judge a book by its cover.

I told her she seemed to be the contradiction of all times. Never, in a million years, would I have guessed that Tina Brown, a publishing legend in her time, a woman famous for gambling her career on pumping new life into fading magazines, tended to keep herself to herself. People imagine that she is the consummate extrovert, the Madonna of magazines.

It was Brown who put a nude, very pregnant Demi Moore on the cover of *Vanity Fair*. The stories she tucked inside the covers were flamboyant, daringly told compulsive adventures involving shocking human behavior. She lets her writers tell the stories sophisticatedly and simply—as if the storyteller is detached and looking at the person, or situation, from a distance. That, of course, isn't true. To appear detached, and have that much information at hand, means that you must get up close and personal.

I told her it didn't make sense. A real introvert could not do her job, at least not the way Tina Brown does the job.

How does she, a self-proclaimed introvert, become the consummate extrovert? How does she switch roles, mindsets? How does she change from demure to dynamic? She spelled it out. She drew pictures for me, wonderful word pictures, and I could see her in action. Introvertedness had limited her. It had disabled her progress. So she forced herself to be a participator rather than an observer.

Her method boiled down to this. She took risks. She dared. She gambled on herself. She forced herself out of passivity and into the pastures of chance.

In case you think this doesn't require guts, think again. The secret that Tina Brown reveals is the secret of stretching, reaching, leaning away from the confines of self and making what you think is impossible, possible. This isn't easy. There has to be something tantalizing, an idea or a focus, on which to pin your hopes. Hers was getting to the top, step by step. She is now in partnership with Miramax Films, an independent Disney-owned production company. Brown is launching a multimedia division centering on a new magazine, movies, and television shows.

When, finally, I asked her to summarize in one simple phrase, the emotional exercise that moved her from where she was to where she wanted to be, she said: "You have to be willing to gamble on yourself."

ॐ Sometimes I have to push against my own nature. I am, in fact, introverted. Many times I purposely do things that are hard to do. That creates tension. That is also professionalism. You do things you're not sure you can do. And there's a whole other side to me. I'm a dreamer. I'm lazy. It's exciting to see your own personality develop under your own duress. It puts you in a driving mode.

Once I posed as a go-go dancer. The best copy you can get is putting yourself in crazy, difficult positions. Professionally, I'd do anything to get a good story. I felt cold being a go-go, dressed in so little. And it was disastrous emotionally. My heart raced. I had a feeling of hysteria. The experience was the antithesis of me. But it was also funny. The great humor was the total disinterest of the men watching. They didn't "watch," they stood around and played pool. Of course I wasn't very good. But the backstage chatter was interesting. Vanilla, an illegal immigrant, was go-go–ing her way across America and she asked me to join her. I suppose if you want to sneer at people, you can. I don't damn or condemn. I just enjoyed the experience. It struck me as farcical. The jokes I made were jokes at myself. Actually, I'm always in a state of hysterical shambles. Outwardly, I appear calm. It's only because I know what I'm doing as an editor.

If I'm shy about telling people their work is no good, the reluctance disappears under the pressure of producing a good magazine ... I'm demanding. I'm appreciative of good people and impatient with people who aren't. I do expect people to do their best and be committed. I hate negativism. It's the one thing I cannot forgive. People who aren't with the venture frustrate me. I like upbeat, enthusiastic people.

I am not a feminist in the sense that I march for the cause. But I strongly feel that women must have their chance. Women are undervalued ... I'm angry about that. I don't, on the other hand, discriminate for women. I hire the best person for the job. In New York, men seem to be frightened of women. Women seem to have become overly aggressive to compensate for their previous sense of being overlooked. The abrasiveness of these women has become intolerable to men. Many men have chosen to opt out of the sexual battle. I'm lucky. My husband is totally non-chauvinistic. It matters to him that I'm satisfied in my career.

I come from a household where the creative project ran

through our house like an artery. The cycle of the artery always involved getting a good review. My mother was a writer. My father was a movie producer and he taught me to admire people who make their own destiny, people who work beyond 9 to 5 to achieve something. I was taught that the effort of the individual shapes a life. You can't expect anything from anybody. You are a unit of one. Ideas are the currency you live by. I adore taking a risk on myself. I like the pressure to succeed or fail. Without pressure, I subside into introversion. Risk is the way I escape my own inhibitions. The essence of the creative buzz is risk. I don't look left or right. Only straight ahead.

Bernadette Peters

on being yourself

It's 10:30 in the morning.

Bernadette Peters, whose tiny frame is wrapped in a pink silk robe, spills out of the bedroom of her New York City hotel suite, wet curls framing her Renaissance face. She has stepped from the shower to the interview. The shower is still running.

A maid, armed with a vacuum cleaner, is humming through her chores. An agent is on the telephone, something about the sensational Bernadette Peters pictures in *Playboy*. And here she is, this little Botticelli blonde, mischief glinting in her eyes, gliding into the room. "Ta-ra! I'm here! Ta-ra!"

She continues a pirouette that is simultaneously elegant and slapstick, then flops into a corner of the couch. The photographer, anxious to freeze the action, instantly follows her with his lens. I have no idea what Steve Martin is doing there. He sees me, a female journalist with a pad and pen, and he is alarmed. "Excuse me," he says gingerly and he disappears, mumbling to no one in particular that he's going back to bed. But he's wearing make-up. Later, Bernadette will explain that Steve had to do a "too early" television show and he's tired.

"Hello," I say. She hesitates too long. "Hello," she says.

Bernadette Peters is a long way from home. This is the ultra-hotel, the upper-crust Carlyle in Manhattan, and she is from a Sicilian family of bakers from Queens. Her family name is Lazzara. Now, at the

Carlyle, you have to be announced to gain entry to her suite. You have to be on her list of visitors to be accepted onto her territory. So I say to Miss Peters: You seem to be very much the individual. "Yes." (Said enthusiastically.) You're a free spirit, aren't you? "Yes." (A giggle precedes the 'yes.') You think it takes courage to be yourself, don't you? "Yes." (Said seriously.) You're a shy show-off, aren't you? "Yes." (She laughs hilariously.) It's hard for you to say "hello," isn't it? "Yes." (This question startles her.)

ॐ Want to know what my big dream in life is? I don't have a five-year plan, a ten-year plan. I don't have specific objectives. My dream is to grow, to be the best I can be. I want to be proud of my work. Maybe marriage. Maybe kids. I said maybe. Then my other dream is to be self-assured. Not to have fears I can't conquer. I am still haunted by fears. Little ones. Oh, I'm shy. I can't make myself say "hello" to a stranger, even if the stranger is someone I'd like to know. You want to know what I do? I practice saying "hello" to strangers.

Acting is a great outlet. On stage I don't have to worry about what I'm doing or saying. In real life you have to worry, yes. You have to ask yourself: have I spoken when I should not have spoken?

My mother always told me I was beautiful. I didn't believe her. I didn't like what I saw in the mirror. I didn't think I was pretty enough or thin enough or popular enough. That was another layer of insecurity, something to be peeled away.

No, I think I am distinctive-looking, different-looking. I don't think I'm gorgeous. At least not in terms of what society thinks is gorgeous. When I love somebody, I love the person that the person is. I love Walter Matthau. To me, he's handsome because of the way he is, not the way he actually looks.

I had another hang-up, still another insecurity that had to

go. I thought that being a success meant that you had to stab someone in the back. The words "career-oriented" and "ambitious"—I used to be afraid of those words. I used to call those words back-stabbing words. Well, now I know ... you don't have to step on or over anybody. Look, I got here in spite of myself. I got here despite all my drawbacks, all my insecurities. Why? Because I don't think of myself in terms of insecurity anymore.

If I hear someone doesn't like me, I say: "Oh, they'll change their mind in the future. Later they'll like me. In two or three years, I'll do something that will make that person like me." I've been hired by people who said, before, that they didn't care for my work.

I've established myself. I know part of this business is rejection. But I know a lot about myself. I can't live in a suburb. I know that just raising a family isn't enough. I've tried to knit. I don't like to knit. I hate to crochet. But I love to act. And I act when I sing. When I'm on stage, when I do something exceptional, something I've never done before, I feel I've been someplace I've never been. And it's all happening inside me.

Yuk—safe is boring. I want to grow. You want to know what creativity is? It's tapping into places you didn't know, places you didn't know existed inside you. You want to know something? It's very limiting to look the way I look. When I started in show business, I wanted to get a job. Any job. So I auditioned for the chorus. Nobody hired me to be a chorus girl. I stuck out too much. I didn't blend. Know what they wanted? A California sunshine orange juice kid. I wasn't like, hey, your well-scrubbed typical American teenager.

Know what I did? I straightened my hair, one of those blunt cuts. I wore collegiate clothes. But my hair was too hard to deal with, all natural curls. And I didn't like the clothes. So I said: "The hell with it." I said: "I am going to be myself." I said: "This is what I am and this is it." See, I didn't care by then. I wasn't getting work the other way, so I decided to be myself. That takes guts. But there's only one of you in the world, so you might as well be the best you can be. Right?

Being an individual is the most important thing in the world. I should have done it all the time. I thought a lot about myself before being myself. Maybe that was a good thing. Individuality is a great release, don't you think? It frees you. You don't have to crunch into somebody else's idea of you, a mold.

It's a matter of stripping away your fears, one by one. We are all layered in fears and they've got to be pulled away. It's like counting backwards, ten, nine, eight ... As the numbers get lower, the peeling away gets easier. You get more and more courage to be yourself. The disappearance of each layer is the very thing that gives you courage.

Julia Child

on setting a good table

So there I was, in the simple boudoir of The French Chef.

Julia Child was tucked in bed, snug and cozy under a king-size calico comforter, a box of tissues at hand ready to catch sneezes and sniffles. Julia had a very bad cold, a very high temperature and a very good tolerance for meeting the press under the most pressing circumstances.

We had spoken several times previously, but always in the kitchen of her rambling old house in the shadow of Harvard Square. Now the flu had come between me and my deadline. Julia is an imperturbable professional. Remember, please, that when she dropped the chicken she was cooking on television, she scooped it up and continued to cook while advising viewers that guests aren't aware of such things. She telephoned me to say that if I wasn't afraid of catching her germs, why not come to her house and interview her in her sickbed? The readers wouldn't know the circumstances of the interview.

The culinary icon was down but not out.

So I drew a chair to the side of Julia's wooden bed. She was on her back, staring at the ceiling, totally relaxed. We were in a darkened room that spoke reams about the power of a Freudian environment, and Julia spoke to me, a disembodied voice.

She said that, in the feminist sense, she was never forced to make a molehill out of a mountain. Technically, that's true. Everything always seemed to work in her favor. Especially her chivalrous, non-chauvinist husband, the late Paul Child, who made his career promoting hers. She sailed through Smith College. She joined the Office of Strategic Services. She studied cuisine in Paris, at L'École des Trois Gourmandes. She built a PBS television career on the cookbook, *Mastering the Art of French Cooking*, and she walked away with an Emmy and international celebrity that continues to escalate.

Meanwhile, feminists who juggled work and housework envisioned the kitchen as a place of incalculable drudge. Their common cry was that cooking was a kind of slavery hoisted on females, especially if it was time-consuming and involved the complications of actual recipes. When I reminded Julia that the feminist population had vociferously downed fashion designers as dictators and the kitchen police as fools, she pretended she'd heard nothing. She blithely spoke of the "joys" of cooking.

We had a friendly little argument about kitchen toil. Her position was simple and to the point: that a home-cooked meal is a civilized setting for good conversation and that cuisine is a creative pursuit. My argument was simple too: If a working woman is lean on time, she's lean on cuisine.

Julia must have given this position a lot of thought. A few weeks later, Julia called my bluff. It started with an out-of-the-blue telephone call inviting me to lunch at her place. Lunch made by Julia Child in Julia Child's home! Oh, my.

So there I was seated at Julia's table and Julia was preparing the meal. She was uncharacteristically silent and I knew instantly that her actions were speaking a thousand words. She took crab meat out of a container, added a bit of mayonnaise, scooped the fish onto a leaf of lettuce sitting on a dish, added a sprig of parsley for decoration, poured me a glass of chilled white wine and said, mischievously, *"Voilà!"*

The preparation procedure, measured in a minute or two, can only be described as speedy. The hilarious part was still to come. "Oh," she said, "there's something in the oven too." With a great flourish, great drama, great showmanship, she produced—toasted slices of French bread wrapped in tinfoil. How we laughed. How wonderful it was.

How glad I was to let her win the debate.

We ate crab meat and drank white wine together and Julia told me that women chefs everywhere wanted equal opportunities in important hotel and restaurant kitchens, that ordinary women had forgotten that the way to a man's heart is through his stomach, that a menu need not be elaborate to taste good. She wanted me to understand her focuses.

Her husband, Paul, became part of our conversation. Julia observed nostalgically that, in the future, it would be nice to think that behind every great woman there was a man. Of course. That's the ideal. But what do male-female relationships have to do with the kitchen?

Julia is such a clever woman. She had an immediate comeback. She told me that all good things begin with cuisine, and I knew hers was the voice of experience.

Years ago, Ernest Hemingway was a friend of ours in Paris. His first wife, Hadley, was a tender woman, lovely, and a good pianist. But Hemingway was jealous and resentful of her talent. It came time for a concert. She was finally going on stage. But Hemingway wouldn't go to his wife's concert. Imagine! She got to the concert hall, the audience was assembled but nothing happened. Finally her agent made an announcement. "Sorry," he said, "Mme. Hemingway is unable to perform." The tickets were refunded.

Hadley was traumatized by the fact her husband wouldn't come to her concert. He was uninterested. He wanted all the attention himself. She didn't play piano for a long time after that. That's a horror story. Paul was exactly the opposite, exactly.

I could have achieved nothing without my husband. He always encouraged me. Always. It's awfully difficult for ambitious women who don't have supportive husbands.

Sometimes I think it would be nice to have some grandchildren. We were sorry we didn't have any children. I was thirty-two when I married. Paul was forty-two. When we finally got around to thinking about children, it was too late. It's too bad. If we had had children, our lives would have been different. But we never had a feeling of a terrible loss. We were too busy.

I'm not a feminist in a militant way. I'm of a different generation. I've never had a struggle. When I got out of college, people didn't question the existing status of women. I wouldn't have gone into a field that didn't welcome women. But I was never threatened or denied because of my sex. Anyway, being big helped. I can't be bullied about.

I wish I'd been smarter in college. I was immature. I didn't take advantage of intellectual opportunities. I should have gone to France and studied French during my junior year. But I really wouldn't want to change anything now because, if I did, nothing would be the same. The older you are, the more you have to draw on in your memory bank.

Maybe more and more men would like to have a capable woman in the kitchen. Feminists should enjoy their kitchens. Kitchens are not places of drudgery ... I love my kitchen. Life centers around the dinner table. A gracious, relaxed atmosphere encourages communication. I think people of all ages should relax over a glass of wine. If you have a glass of wine, you don't need martinis. And children probably wouldn't be using drugs if they had a happy home life. A happy home centers around a happy table.

We have a house in the south of France. We've had it for twenty-five years. When we went there, Paul would paint. I would cook and write. We would visit restaurants. I love France. France is foreign. In France, you know you're somewhere else. The French can be prickly but they're intelligent. I love the old streets, the old buildings, the ancient medieval smells. The subways in Paris smell like burned paper. The countryside is beautiful. And everywhere you see people at lunch who take great care in ordering. They want to know how the food is being cooked. It's not fast food at all.

I'm fascinated by food, even the mechanics of preparing it. Food is an art form. It's both manual and intellectual. Then there's the spiritualism of it, the creativity and harmony. You create a taste. You present an image on a plate. You always try to be different. It doesn't have to be an invention. It just has to be original.

I don't welcome failure, especially if it happens in public. I have failed. In food there are complete failures, like the fallen soufflé. But failures are valuable. It's terribly important to know the pitfalls—and I do.

Claire Bloom

on stretching

Long ago, the British press dubbed her "little mouse."

They didn't mean that the world-famous actress Claire Bloom is a mousy gray character with a blah personality. Her mousiness is a reference to her whispery ways, her first and inaccurate impression of overwhelming docility. Even when she is wearing boots made for stomping, her studied stride is soundless. That in itself is a dead giveaway. Her seeming acquiescence to all things quiet, makes her the observer rather than the observed. And what an observer she is.

When I told her there was a method in her madness, she hushed her laughter and it manifested itself only as a sly smile.

Claire describes herself as "cautious"—"Cautious Claire," she sing-songs. Caution, she tells me, is an underrated protective mechanism. Well, I say to Claire, you couldn't be cautious and be the great actress you are. You've played hysterical door-slammers, raging alcoholics and reckless nymphomaniacs. Cautious Claire never seems cautious in the limelight. Well, she counters facetiously, all women should be cautious but, by the same token, know when to throw caution to the wind.

Exactly what does throwing caution to the wind feel like?

Claire searches for a word. "Stretching," she says.

Her answer seems too elementary, too trite. Claire, I say, what you probably mean is that you throw your vulnerableness to the wind, forget it, deny it, replace it, substitute it with a strength, even a faked strength, and thus you become something else, someone else—your stronger self?

"Exactly," she says. "That's stretching."

An actor's stretch, from passive to powerful, may appear to be a universe apart from everyday living, everyday careers. But all the world's a stage. Women dress the part, play the part, act the part of their chosen professions. They, too, have a professional life. They, too, have to stretch. They too have to step on the stage of their careers. They too have vulnerableness that makes them ache inside. They too have the fear of rejection, of failing. In the sphere of self-empowerment, "stretching" is universal of womanhood.

Ironically, my mother defined "stretching" in the same language as Claire. "You must play the part," my mother told me. "Imagine yourself on your stage, stretched to the limits of your best self." Whenever an interview goes beyond mere questions and answers, when it is stretched into intimate conversation, the exchange of experiences are blurred. The tapestry of the conversation is rich with feelings.

I defined my concept of stretching for Claire:

To stretch beyond what you perceive to be your most vulnerable is to assume an inner strength you didn't know existed. You pretend to be more forceful, more brave, than you really are. It begins as an act. But the make-believe feels right, and your heart tells you what your brain never did: that fictional feelings entrenched in positiveness take root and become part of your emotional arsenal. The little mouse roars. I wanted to succeed? I dressed for success. I wanted to write? I wrote stories that were printed but for which I wasn't paid. I wanted to move up, be promoted? I did the first menial tasks better than anybody, faster and more efficiently. I got good notices.

Claire listened with her inner ear and, taking her turn, she defined stretching.

    If you stop stretching, everything in your life stops. This year I decided to do things on my own. Writing is something you do alone. You rely only on yourself. The same goes for the one-woman Shakespeare readings. I said to myself: "Create things on your own. Don't worry about being an employed actress." I said: "Cook things up for yourself." I've always been dependent on outside forces. For once, I wanted to call the plays for myself. And I've done things I never thought I could do.

Nothing good ever happens to you if you don't stretch. Stretching is pleasant. I feel obliged to stretch because without stretching life would be boring. Depression is a by-product of being bored. I have a tremendous sense about not wasting time. Think of the choice. Either you use your time or you die.

Acting is a gamble. You don't what will come. It's a career full of suspense. It means life has to change. The trick is to cope with the changes. Coping is everything. I suppose, somewhere inside me, there's a strength. When I was younger, I used to get in a terrible state when things went wrong. But I was like bedsprings. Push me down and I popped back up. It's terribly important to be resilient.

I've always liked to gamble. That's a great deal of my values, daring. When you do a one-woman show, there's absolutely no one to control your interest. There's not even a prompter. If you go wrong, there's no one to blame. But you've got to start off in a modest way, take small steps at a time. I didn't just leap into the Shakespeare show ... I started off quietly, in a protected environment, among friends. If I had taken a big leap and done it in a big way at first, it would have been frightening. It was like putting my foot in the water, going one step at a time, getting wet slowly.

I have stage fright, especially when I realize that everything depends on me. But I have a saving grace: a character. I disappear into it. That's the pleasure. You are still you, but are also somebody else. It's almost as if you step out of yourself, you watch yourself creating an effect.

I used to be self-conscious, but I had to get over that. Somehow I grew up and I realized it was an unnecessary burden I was carrying. I just decided not to be self-conscious anymore. And I wasn't. I could always rely on my mother for advice.

She put me in my place when I got off the track. She made one thing clear to me: I must not do anything second-rate. "Better to stop than to be second-rate," my mother would say. There was always the reminder to pursue excellence.

I have made errors in judgment. I have regretted them. When you make an error, you wait, you try to straighten yourself out. You can be shaken. This is especially true of professional mistakes. You accept a play. It doesn't go; you're out of work for a long time. You are left high and dry. Literally. You pay even dearer for personal mistakes ... the thing about mistakes is not to be debilitated by them.

First you've got to rid yourself of negative feelings. Go to an exercise class. Do yoga. Yoga is a wonderful thing. It calms you down enormously. It centers you. But knocks are hard to take, and it's foolish to say they're not.

If a play is rejected, I tell myself that I am not rejected. But rejection in private life is worse. Divorce is the worst thing that can happen to anybody. Divorce and the death of someone you love are the two worst things. After a tremendous shock, it's wise not to do anything, to be quiet. You have to regroup your focus. I get strength from inside myself. I have one—no, two good friends. They are precious to me. When there are bad times, some friends kick you. But that's how you find out who your friends are.

When Laurence Olivier was married to Vivian Leigh, I stayed with them in their home outside London. I was appearing in a play and I got a dreadful notice. I was very upset, distraught. Olivier took me for a walk and said: "You should see the review I got in *Romeo and Juliet*." He showed it to me. It wasn't good. Olivier said you can only be perfect once in every ten years.

What happens is that you draw the line and then you take a step (forward), a really good step and you say to yourself: "That wasn't (so) bad."

Carrie Fisher

on being funny and smart

She's not Princess Leia of *Star Wars*.

She's not the propositioner in *Shampoo*.

Carrie Fisher is five feet small. Her reddish hair is squeaky clean and it's cut geometrically, as if she were dressed for a boarding school in England. Her shapeless smock, the color of lilac, is collared with an embroidered bib. It is reminiscent of something you'd find in a kiddie boutique. Carrie is in caricature.

Adamantly she refuses to be photographed before, during or after the interview. She doesn't want the world to see her like this, in baby doll's clothes. Still, she admits her greatest childhood wound: "I always wondered if it all happened because I was bad." Carrie was two years old when her father, Eddie, left her mother, Debbie, to marry Liz Taylor. Everything about Carrie seems deliberately childish, as if she is forever tethered to her past.

So what makes Carrie Fisher tick?

Ah-ha, she says, pointing her forefinger at me, that's what she has spent her whole life discovering amid the rubble and ruin of the romantic melodrama of her parents' love, marriage, and war. I tell her I know who she is: a fine writer and a fine actress. She knows it's a tease. No comment. I tell her I know she dropped out of Beverly Hills High School, at fifteen, to dance in the chorus of her mother's Broadway hit musical, *Irene*. No comment.

"I'm funny," she proclaims.

Give me proof, I say.

She mentions her one-room log cabin in the Hollywood Hills.

What's funny about that?

"It's my sane asylum," she says.

I mention that she is a wildly successful author (*Postcards from The Edge*). No comment. I congratulate her on the fact that Mike Nichols, genius, made a movie based on her book of the same name, and let her write the script. No comment. This is all very well and good, but she's got bigger things going for her.

"I'm smart," she says, and this time she hands me proof of her own volition. Carrie overdosed on drugs in 1985 and was rushed to the emergency room at Cedars Sinai Medical Center, and "I bottomed out. I'm talking rock bottom. I was frightened. I didn't want to die, so I paid attention to myself. I found out how not to do drugs. I was thorough. I didn't want this to ever happen to me again."

Then, for emphasis, she repeats herself. "Smart."

We talk about how these two yardsticks, smartness and funniness, are the ultimate measures of how other people see you and, most of all, how you see yourself.

     Most of the time I feel like an outsider. I feel like I'm missing a vital piece of information about fitting in. I don't know how to feel connected ... I use humor to gain acceptance. Humor is my survival. Humor is my coping mechanism.

It's exhausting to spend time worrying about what it would be like if things were different. Now I accept things the way they are. I swear it has a lot to do with aging. I don't agonize so much. Anxiety and youth go together. I've done a lot of therapies. A lot of information has lodged in my brain. I know about possibilities and acceptance.

But here's my dumbness. I think with my mouth. I think out the answers to questions out loud. I enjoy verbal deduction. I can think on my feet—or yours. I'm glib. But I don't insult people.

Suppose I'm with someone who's not straightforward, someone who says one thing and means another, someone who
holds a double conversation. I get very direct. Being direct in
this kind of situation is intimidating. Then glibness becomes
worthwhile.

I have a love-hate relationship with everything. Recently, I
had a talk with my ex-husband [singer-songwriter Paul Simon]
on this very same subject. I said: "I used to want to be smart.
Now I am smart. Now I want to be clear, precise."

But, don't you see? There's no truth. I see all the sides of a
situation. I love that. What I hate is that I can't figure things
out precisely. My ex-husband reminded me that there will always be different ways of looking at the same things. I told
him what I'm going to tell you: "That's the trouble."

I'm not self-obsessed. Self-obsessed means me, me, me. I'm
interested in other people. I've obsessed with projects. If I do
something, I do it wholeheartedly My mother says I shut everything out. I'm not overwired. Oh, sometimes I feel like a
nine-year-old kid in a toy store. I have a lot of intense energy.
But my energy isn't fractured. It's focused. I wear myself out
writing.

I am much analyzed. I've been in therapy since I was fifteen. I had to learn not to blame anybody else for my troubles.
It was sad. I had to turn my back on myself, go inward.

I come from a family of epic personalities. My parents are
big, colorful, expressive. They're celebrities. Famous people
are famous because they have inherent charisma. Both my
parents have that. But there's more. They know how to get
attention. When that's done well, when it doesn't appear that's
what they're doing, it can be very powerful.

I don't feel I'm as beautiful as my mother. I never thought
I could ever be that beautiful. Early on I figured I'd better get
something else going. I'm not unattractive. But I've compen-
sated. I'm funny. I'm smart.

My marriage lasted less than a year. My ex-husband and I

wanted to be together. We tried to make the relationship work, so we got married. Wrong reason to get married, right? I don't know what went wrong. How can you explain those things? Maybe the way I am isn't conducive to a conventional relationship. It just doesn't work out.

I'm uncomfortable with sentiment. If someone else is sentimental, I'm expected to respond in kind. That's embarrassing. It makes me feel awkward. Even when I write about emotions, I do it in an unsentimental way. I like describing feelings without saying what the feeling feels like.

Jihan Sadat

on widowhood

Jihan Sadat looks fragile, in need of protection. Indeed, there's an armed bodyguard lurking in the shadows, and at her side is another British-educated Arab gentleman who is fluent in several languages. He, too, is probably a bodyguard disguised as the interview auditor. He thrusts his right hand in his right-hand jacket pocket. It is bulging with more than a fist.

Mrs. Sadat weighs and sorts her words carefully. When she speaks of women caught in the revolving door of widowhood, and their wish to emerge from the chrysalis of grief into the real world, her thoughts are very personal and they're sculpted in simplicity. But she is a complicated woman living in a complicated situation. What is distracting is her spun-sugar appearance. She looks like the Middle Eastern equivalent of the Southern belle: pampered, coiffed, manicured, her glamour enhanced cosmetically. Even her suit screams the best of Paris couture. She is a beautiful woman who touts her beauty.

But there's more to her than meets the eye.

Mrs. Sadat is not a politician. But she has been quietly politicking for women's rights in the Moslem culture. She is a role model of what much of her female constituency idealizes: pretty, educated, vocal, commanding respect. Which probably explains why there are bodyguards around. What she has to say is not popular with the fanatics who blew her husband, Egyptian president Anwar Sadat, to bits.

To understand the real Mrs. Sadat is to understand that she is the feminine counterpart, and an intrinsic blend, of what her husband used to be. She is a rebel. She is a reconnoiterer. She is a reconciler.

Rebel:

When she was fifteen years old, Jihan married Anwar Sadat, very much against her parents' wishes. He was eighteen years her senior, jobless, divorced and a recently-released political prisoner who had been tossed into jail for his "nationalistic activity." Not exactly the man of her parents' choice. Jihan, like Anwar, was a classic rebel, a teenager who shunned outside control. This, in fact, is what Jihan and Anwar liked about each other. They pledged allegiance to one another. The two rebels merged their power. They became a formidable Mr. & Mrs.

Reconnoiterer:

Even when she was engulfed in an emotional jail of grief, a widow whose terrible circumstances of instant widowhood are not unlike Jackie Kennedy's or Ethel Kennedy's, she forced herself to assess her strengths and minimize her weaknesses. She went on with her life despite a barrage of chauvinistic criticisms rooted in the military. There were bodyguards around because she was talking to me on the record. That, in itself, was as brave as her words.

Reconciler:

How had she come to terms and made peace with her husband's murder and her widowhood, but also with the idea that she, a woman alone, could stare into the face of her hostile Arab male world and pacify the skepticism, even veiled threats, while at the same time satisfying her own needs of independence?

Jihan Sadat told me how she made a molehill out of her mountain.

    I don't live in the past. I have learned to live only for the moment. When I have something to do, a project, I put aside all my problems, all my memories and concentrate only on what I'm doing.

Just before the assassination happened, I said to myself:

"There are fanatics out there." And then the shooting. The memories are still hard to bear.

I overcame the tragedy by feeling I did work that would please my husband. My children cried. They often cried. I said to them: "Don't cry. Let him see us going on, going forward." I never let my children feel their mother was weak and sad. They lost their father. I was courageous because I didn't want them to think they were losing me.

To go back to school [Cairo University and the University of South Carolina] was a very big effort. But I wanted to set a good example for Egyptian women. Actions speak louder than words. Finding time to go to school was very difficult because I had a busy schedule. I had to settle for less sleep.

The other difficult thing was that all the professors had high expectations for me. I always felt that I had to live up to those expectations. But I truly believe in what I was doing. Just because my husband died, just because there was so much grief, didn't mean I should stop. I have decided to keep on working until I, too, die.

I'm criticized in the press in Egypt. In fact, the whole Arab world. The fanatics criticize me. The fanatics are against improvements. The fanatics insist a woman's place is in the home. To them I say: "This is not a women's battle against men. It's a way to build a better society together. Women are the other half of a couple. Women are the other half of the population."

There is progress in Egypt but not enough. There's not enough progress anywhere. That's what keeps me going.

When my husband died, I could have said "enough." But I never feel I've done enough for women's rights.

The Koran stipulates that the man who has more than one wife must treat all wives equally. Maybe he will give them all the same amount of money, but always, one is his favorite. The new law [1979] is that the divorced woman automatically gets the house. Real estate is prized in Egypt, so it's not so easy to divorce a wife anymore. Now the husband has to pay alimony. This is progress.

My husband and I really understood each other. We were two partners who completed one another. I never interfered with his work. He never interfered with mine. I was fifteen when I married him. He was just out of prison. He was devoted to Egypt. I loved his personality. I insisted on marrying him. My mother didn't approve. But, finally, she agreed. It wasn't easy to go ahead and to marry under these circumstances. But there were never any regrets. My mother finally accepted him completely.

I believe love can work miracles. The best thing in life is to love and be loved. Love is the only thing that lasts.

Suzanne Somers

on alcoholism

A bed wetter and a thumb sucker, at thirteen. An affair with a man old enough to be her father, at sixteen. Pregnant, then married, at seventeen. Divorced, at eighteen. Single mother with a son, at nineteen. These milestones preceded an affair with an older man, someone to whom she refers to only as "Mr. Bates," and, later, an arrest for writing a rubber check. You can practically identify each year of Suzanne Somers' young life by a tumble of one kind of awful crisis or another.

What saved Somers was long and intense in-your-face therapy.

She forced herself to confront her old repressions, snatch the monsters from her recesses, examine them microscopically as cancer cells of the soul, call them by their real name: badly diseased self-esteem.

Somers, who has a long stretch of blond hair and whose body is shaped like a long string bean with a bosom, can trace all her worst troubles to one man: her father, an Irish immigrant brewery worker. He had one problem that wrecked his life and, by association, hers: alcoholism. It twisted her childhood, girlhood and early teenage years into an environment of terror.

Either she is a born actress or she was born to act.

When her father's drunken rampages exploded, she first locked herself in a closet, and then she double-locked herself in the closet of her imagination. She pretended she was onstage and the slaps she heard were claps of applause. When she got a little older, she looked for love in all the wrong places. Eventually she met a person who changed the tenor of her life and her lifestyle: a psychologist. The lesson of life that she learned was lost father love cannot be replaced by romantic love. One is not the substitute for the other.

It was the therapist, her savior, who asked two questions over and over: Why do you expect so little from life? Why do you expect so little from your love relationships? Her therapist taught her the art of "visualization," the idea that you not only dream the best of everything for yourself, you actually "see" it on the screen of the brain's computer. Once Somers had a clear vision of who she was and what she could be, she decided "to take the world by storm." Nothing was going to stand in her way. No one was going to stand in her way.

By the time I met Suzanne Somers, she was a superstar. She seemed sure of herself, very sophisticated in an expensive black suit, very suave. She reigned over her elegant Four Seasons Hotel suite. It was as if she'd been to the manor born. When she dismissed the uniformed maid and room service waiter hovering around her, I asked all the hard questions of her past.

She never flinched.

Somers is that rare breed of woman whose marshmallow fluff is forged from steel. It's not the steel of chilliness. What she has is the steel of experience translated into a strength-of-self.

So I asked Somers if there was one pivot around which her metamorphosis had revolved?

Yes, yes, she said. It was the magic of forgiveness. She said the relief of forgiveness is overwhelming and transforming. Without meaning to, she sounded like a Somers version of the Lord's Prayer. She made it sound as if her trespasses had been forgiven because she had forgiven him who trespassed against her.

    The phrase, "low self-esteem," sounds trite. But without confidence, you can accomplish nothing. I had no idea I had talent. I had no idea that I had a nice personality. I thought I wasn't as good as anyone else. I saw no potential in myself. It all came from the shame and embarrassment of living with a drunken father. I felt isolated.

I was the one child who didn't drink. But something was wrong with me. I was constantly in emotional and financial trouble. I chose a married man to love. I accepted being No. 2 in his life.

When I was in jail for the bounced check, I realized how precious free will is. When the jail door slammed shut, my low self-esteem hit me in the face. I didn't cry. I had a sense of desperation. I had botched up my life. I just sat there with my head in my hands.

I didn't drink, but I was at the bottom. Maybe I would have committed suicide. I don't know. But I did think: "This world would be better off without me." Alcoholism kills. It ends in death or insanity unless you get help.

When I finally went into therapy, the therapist pointed out my patterns of behavior. I had created my own crises. Slowly, but surely, this did me in.

The therapist showed me my worth. She told me all the good things about me. All I ever heard at home was what was wrong with me. From session to session, I began to understand that alcoholism was my father's problem, not mine. I became convinced that I could help myself.

One day, I said: "That's it. I've made mistakes. But I can do better." I had been badly affected by growing up in a dysfunctional family. I started to undo the past by confronting it. I peeled away the layers to clarity.

I was bent on survival. I had lived in a little white house that was all darkness inside. I used to put on a happy face when I left there. I pretended life was as pretty as the outside of our house. Once I understood my own worth, I put on a happy face for real. It wasn't a conscious effort anymore.

The clincher was the moment I realized I was a victim of my father's disease.

I had always wanted to be different, not ordinary. My father was a drunk from the day I was born. As a child, when I felt the pain of disharmony, I fantasized. I sat in a closet. I hid in small, dark, safe places. I pretended I was a movie star. I pretended people liked me. I pretended I heard clapping. This was my escape.

Dreams are very potent. People define themselves in their dreams. I had practiced what psychologists call visualization. I had seen pictures of myself in my head. Later, when I got well, I decided that nothing was going to get in my way.

I wasn't afraid of failure. Failure was no big deal. Failure could not be as bad as the life I had experienced. I said: "I'm going for it."

As a child of an alcoholic, I was left out. This is important. I thought that's what I deserved. When I was having an affair with Alan, a married man, I felt I deserved to be left out of his life. I accepted being No. 2 to his wife and family. I felt worthless. I felt shame. But I loved him and I couldn't help myself. Yet it was as if I was living out my father's prediction of me.

Now, looking back, I think I did an admirable job of surviving with the tools I was given. When I was fourteen, I was expelled from school. The Mother Superior found some love notes in my locker. I had fantasies about a boy. It was just a young girl's crush. I had written him love notes that I was never going to send. There was form and substance to those letters. They were yearnings from my heart. I wish my writing had been encouraged. The Mother Superior told me she wasn't happy with either me or my grades. She told me I was "cheap trash."

I believed her.

In retrospect, I realize I was starved for love. I wanted acceptance. When I was sixteen, I had an affair with a man the age of my father. He was a father figure. I wanted love and affection from my father. I didn't get it.

I loved my father and I hated him. My family was an alcohol-centered family, not a child-centered family. I never stood up to my father and said: "You can't do this." I just thought: "If

I was a better child, maybe he wouldn't act this way."

But, once, my father ripped up all my clothes. I hit him hard on the head with a tennis racket. He had a concussion and had to get eight stitches. Later I realized that the gesture of violence was based on my first expression of self-esteem. Maybe I was thinking: "You can't do this to me and get away with it." At the time, though, I felt guilty.

I had a broken heart. My mother had a broken heart. She thought she had failed as a wife. I felt I had failed as a human being. Unless you get help, you can walk around with a broken heart for the rest of your life. I had to get to the point where I understood that life is what you make it. Life isn't what you were. It's what you are. Now I have everything I've ever wanted.

I feel deserving because I made my success happen. My success was getting well. Alcoholism is a disease, like cancer. My father has allowed me to go public with our story. To me, that makes him a great man. Forgiving is hard. I have forgiven my father. The relief of that forgiveness is overwhelming.

Jane Pauley

on priorities

Even before I met Jane Pauley, I loved her graceful battlefield attitude. She always seemed to know when to buck and whom to buck without appearing to be a bucker. I had also loved the intelligence and grace she beamed across the small screen and then, when we met, I discovered that all that feisty shine is real.

Jane Pauley was ensconced behind her cluttered desk at NBC-TV headquarters at 30 Rockefeller Plaza. The couch to her left was filled with toys, handmade gifts from viewers for her twins. Toys in the office were the real reminders, symbols, of the fact that she has two lives: camera and off-camera—and one must not detract from, or become more important than, the other.

Pauley, one of the highest-paid women on television, is married to her career. She jumped from the news anchor desk at WMAQ-Chicago to a network job. She succeeded Barbara Walters in 1976, putting in eight years on the *Today* show and garnering an audience of five million people. And she's also married to *Doonesbury* cartoonist Garry Trudeau, with whom she has a family. The enormous demands of her big-time television career could have canceled out love and the demands of the Trudeau marriage which carries its own set of time and energy claims.

It hasn't.

Pauley has mastered the art of juggling. She is both a happy professional and a happy wife and mother. We talked a lot about happiness: what it is, how you get it, how you keep it. I told her that I've always admired women who move beyond restrictions and constrictions, women who buck the system they're stuck in and emerge winners within the system they buck. Inevitably, everything we talked about involved the idea of having specific priorities.

Pauley is beautiful. When she laughs, she is more beautiful. When I called her a "bucker-juggler," she laughed and said nothing good in life is ever accomplished if you don't have priorities. Without priorities, there is confusion and, in an atmosphere of sustained confusion, progress is stunted.

Pauley is a master of this kind of perspective. She can look at the whole of something, especially her own life, see all the precise parts separately and make them fit. She evaluates everything in terms of their interrelation. Yet she has a definable point of view about everything. She believes, and I do, that the clarity of life starts with the clarity of self. You have to be clear about everything: every move, every response, every detail.

My main question to Pauley, couched in a million smaller questions, was simply: How have you done it? How have you managed to be a television superstar, with an audience of millions and a salary to match, while succeeding in a man-woman partnership with a famous man and, further, being a good mom?

The essence of her reply was so revealing, so illuminating, that I almost didn't write it down because I was fascinated with her honest plain-talk about the importance of prioritization. Jane Pauley is madly in love with Garry Trudeau, but within the context of career, she gave credit where credit was due: to herself.

"Garry doesn't have a direct hand in my interviews, but he has influenced the quality of my work," she said, looking me straight in the eye. "He is an important factor in my career. But remember, I got here without him."

I remember! Oh, how I remember that Pauley even bucked the popular impression that the great Trudeau, her marital partner and the big background presence of her life, had not had a huge hand in her continuing success. Instead she bolstered the reality that she, a woman alone, had forged her own career.

I'm aware of my priorities. Family comes first. Maybe I would not have said that before the children arrived. I was happily married. But a couple is not a crowd. It has been implied that I'm involved in part-time motherhood because I have a full-time job. When it was just Garry and me, my work came first. I would never have asked my husband the pointed question: "Which is more important, me or your career?" But, with babies, it's a different question. Babies come first because they're so needy. Having admitted that to you, I also admit that I have to juggle the reality of my employer's expectations.

Employers don't negotiate family crises. I'm expected to be here. Priorities then become a touchy, different question ... I've simplified my life a lot. It's work and home and home and work.

My husband doesn't feel a need to be a celebrity. He feels his work speaks for him. He has a profound public voice and his comic strip panels contain less than thirty words. He feels he doesn't need the trappings of celebrity. I'm not exactly wallowing in celebrity, but I have a higher public profile than Garry. I don't deliver a commentary on television. I deliver me. My comments are not as important as his. But they are more personal.

He [Garry] is inclined to say my work has more credibility with him than it does with me. Garry would not have married a woman without ambition. When I go through periods of fantasy about giving up television for motherhood, he respects the profundity of my nurturing instincts. He also has a realistic view of how much I am defined by my career. If I gave it up, there would be a void in my life. In the long run, my career is important to me.

Unfortunately, I don't have the kind of career in which I can take off a year. One of my gifts is to repress the paranoia connected to this job. I have one of the best jobs in broadcasting, if not the best. I'm in a priority position [currently co-anchor of *Dateline: NBC*]. There are a lot of people who'd like this job, let alone the compensation that comes with it. It is an enviable place to be. Over the years, there have been any number of women who I've read (in newspaper columns) being groomed to take my place. There's always another public reminder about the tenuousness of my career. When I signed my contract, it didn't contain the clause, "'Til death do us part."

Some people have plotted and conspired against me. I've always gone blithely along, ignoring it. I've been lucky. I didn't politic my way into this business ... I didn't engineer it. But the issue I face is: If I do not deliver the performance I am paid to deliver, I would be out in no time flat. The people most threatening to my career have been the men who tinker with the show. There have been times I didn't know how dangerous the atmosphere was until the danger was past.

When I went on my honeymoon, I almost lost my job ... I didn't even hear the rumblings. I had gone blissfully on my honeymoon. When I returned, the danger was over. I simply was able to keep my job. My boss has always said the minute they find someone better to do my job, that person will have my job. But I have not spent time fending off potential adversaries. I've spent my time preparing myself to do the job.

Every now and then, if I feel vulnerable, I go home, crawl into bed, assume the fetal position, pull the covers over my head and stay there. It's called the panic of anxiety. Or I'll race to Garry, pound my fist on his chest and panic verbally. After that, I feel fine. But Garry is a basket case on my behalf. You see, I transfer all my anxieties on him.

I've always had plenty of love in my life. I need love. I had my babies and when they were brought to me in the hospital, I fell in love with them immediately. Married love is a safety net. Now I have someone to come home to.

When I was blossoming or ballooning [during pregnancies], my boss speculated that I was doing my best work. He said that because I had an enriched home life, I had the confidence to take risks. It spilled over to my career.

Judy Collins

on amazing grace

Judy Collins has been a wretch. She knows what it's like to be lost and found. She knows what it's like to be blind and have your vision restored. She knows all about starting over, and thanking God for opening your eyes to recognize opportunity. When she speaks of the word *opportunity*, she sings it from a smile and her tone is strictly Mary Sunshine: "Op...por...tun...ity!"

The thing about Judy Collins is that she likes to accentuate the positive—not in a Pollyanna way, but in the sense of creating Opportunity where there is none. She personifies Amazing Grace.

The song celebrates the pure joy of recognizing new visions, new chances, new life and being able to cull new realizations, new wisdom, from bad happenings. It's about threshing wheat from the chaff of life and celebrating your ability to do so.

When Judy sings "Grace," she is singing the song of her true self.

Collins had a bout with polio when she was ten, a bout with tuberculosis and a charity ward when she was twenty-one. She struggled with alcohol and LSD. She had an abortion. She watched her ex-husband gain custody of their son. And probably the worst: having a benign blood-vessel tumor removed from a vocal cord and worrying that the surgery would destroy her singing ability. But it wasn't cancer, and she went on to record six gold record albums for a big-time record company.

Then, after twenty-four years, she was fired without warning. She was told that her style, now a classic, was not what the company wanted anymore. Collins felt as if she'd been dropped from a tall building onto the pavement. She was dead. Only she was alive. For awhile, she didn't know how to get up and get going again. She was in an emotional coma.

Then this simple thought invaded her psyche: "Maybe I don't have to be satisfied with 'no.'"

It's one thing to tell yourself that the "no" you've been handed isn't final. It's quite another to take a "no" and fashion it into a "yes!" How did she close the gap between the negative and the positive?

Collins said she manufactured an "irrational confidence" in herself. I said: "What's that?" She said: "A burning optimism." I said: "What do you mean?" She said: "It's trusting your heart in everything. Your subconscious meets your conscious and you become your best self. You're at your most powerful." I said: "So it's when you were blind and now you have x-ray vision. You can see through things, around things, between things."

"Amazing Grace?" I said.

"Amazing Grace," she said.

    I was in total shock. The new executive of my old record company just said: "You're not being renewed. You're no longer our type." I felt wounded.

I tried to see some other possibility from the disaster. Eventually, I sat down at a computer and wrote about my feelings, it's how I processed what had happened to me. It was a relief. But it was also an emotional recourse. I thought: Maybe I don't have to be satisfied with "no."

Everybody is given constraints. A constraint is a limitation, a parameter. Sometimes a constraint is a crisis. Constraints seem to be rejections, dead ends, deprivations. My father [Charles Collins, a musician who had his own radio show] was blind. But he felt blindness was the impetus that made him want to be more. Blindness is a constraint. He saw blindness as a tool.

I knew I had to begin again. I had all kinds of fears. Still do. I fear success. I fear failure. I fear not remembering the words to my songs on stage. A predominant fear is that I'll lose my voice. I had a growth removed from my vocal cord. I thought it was cancer. It wasn't. Sometimes I have to get my fears to go up in flames.

I have a spiritual guide, a muse. That muse is myself. She sees what I see. She does what I do. If I give her a bad time, she gives me a bad time. If I give her a break, she gives me a break. I court my muse in a pragmatic way. I rest. I eat well. I stay well and she stays well.

I had an abortion in 1961. I was, in fact, having something done that was illegal. I was in no condition, financially or emotionally, to provide for a child. I was not in a crisis of conscience. But I was terrified. The doctor was brusque. I was by myself, alone and isolated. Abortion is the right of women. I'm not speaking of an issue about which I know nothing. The abortion experience has united me with women everywhere who have had abortions, even kitchen abortion.

When I was ten years old, I had a polio attack. I was in the hospital, but—and I can't explain this—I had a raw conviction I'd be all right. It was an irrational confidence because I was part of the polio plague. Yet I had a burning optimism. I trusted my heart.

When I was twenty-one, I didn't have any money. I was sick. I had a fever. My symptom was gurgling lungs. I had TB. I was a charity case in a hospital. I stayed there four months. When I was at the hospital, I lost custody of my son. I was in an enforced holding pattern. I couldn't go anywhere. It was a time of reflection and determination. I practiced the guitar. I wrote in my journals. I wrote music. I moved within the interior of myself. Outside, there was chaos. But I took advantage of the quiet, the stillness, the schedule of the hospital. I trusted my heart.

I struggled later on, with LSD and alcohol. I had problems with relationships. A man left me after I thought we were enjoying an okay relationship. I found it hard to keep going. I started drinking when I was working. I struggled with therapists.

None of them seemed to think I had a drinking problem. They were all willing to give me uppers, downers, and sleeping pills. Finally, one therapist said: "You have a problem. It's not going away unless you make it go away." I thought: "You're either going to get better or die." It was an either-or situation.

I made a conscious decision not to die. I went into treatment. I rethought things. I came to understand that I had a choice. I chose to lead a healthy life.

Then I began to accept myself and my situation. I accepted my vulnerabilities and limitations. I learned when to say "no." When I became at ease with myself, I became at ease with the world.

Choice. That's always the key.

Long ago, when I was little, I learned that there's a kind of sanctity to being a performer. You have to protect your creative machinery. Sometimes, restoration of the creative spirit is found in seclusion, separating yourself from intrusions.

Diana Vreeland

on pizzazz

A female Cardinal, looking like a living Dante wearing a red chemise, is seated ramrod-straight and formidably sure, behind a desk sprouting a neat row of burning incense candles. This is the only light in the room. The drapes are drawn and the natural light of the sun is shut out. I am in Satan's den. It's a New York City office somewhere-on-high.

The fiery glow of the candles wave flickering shadows that dance across the walls of this red room and drench it in the smoky, heady, eye-stinging scent associated with old-world cathedrals. Without a word, the dweller of this roost had spelled out an undeniable fact. She was not a wishy-washy, think-pink person. The office is a red rectangle awash with the color of hell and blood. The red is relieved only by the quiet roar of leopard carpeting.

I am about to interview Diana Vreeland, the supernatural fashion legend who, even in death, is a mythic icon. It is the early '70s. Vreeland is the much-feared, much watched, much-envied editor-in-chief of *Vogue*, the high priestess whose word, spoken or written, was the last word. The bloated power she wrought was enormous.

Vreeland was so enamored of red, so obsessed by it, that she had slashed her sunken cheeks with it and exaggerated the pout of her homely, hard-edged lips with it. Her sprayed-to-death coiffure, the color of black boot polish, hugged her head like a helmet with bangs.

Everyone knows how Diana is pronounced. Forget Princess Di. Paris-born Vreeland, a fashion priestess who pulsated with an unquenchable penchant for theatricality, pronounced it "Dee-ahh-nah." You were expected to assume the same pseudo speech inflection if—big if—you were given permission to address The Legend by her first name. She always thought that Dee-ahh-nah was the appropriate salutary homage to her position in life.

Vreeland did not like interviews because interviews put the interviewer in the driver's seat. She was a control freak. But she had agreed to be interviewed. I thought this was going to be one of my proudest (exclusive) newspaper coups.

There had been photographs of bare-breasted African tribeswomen in *Vogue*. This had nothing to do with Fashion. Or did it? I thought Vreeland was championing a trend toward the unfettered female body, that she was making a symbolic statement supporting the women's liberation movement that was calling for emancipation from old ties. Then there were the photo layout of exotic flowers shown one-by-one, in single splendor. Was this an eloquent statement of the changeless allure of simplicity? Of the idea that less is more?

Vreeland's bold, and refreshingly new, editorial stance was impressive and trend-setting. Other fashion magazines were beginning to mimic her editorial approach which seemed steeped in symbolism.

I had no inkling whatsoever that the row of burning incense candles constituted a red-hot warning not to wander too close to her professional politics and, if you did, it was at your own risk. I eliminated warm-up preliminaries. I asked "why?" about the African tribeswomen and the "why?" of the single-flower layout.

Vreeland's retort was blunt, snarly, swift and non-negotiable. "Out!" she hissed impetuously, pointing to the door. I couldn't help but notice that her Fu Manchu red fingernails matched the room.

Still, the shock of being bounced paralyzed me. I was unable to move. No wonder Vreeland used to tell people that her last name began with V and that V stood for Violent. She repeated herself in a crescendo: "Out! Out!"

When I was finally able to gather my strength and walk out into the sunshine of Madison Avenue which, in a fit of depression, I likened to the boulevard of broken dreams, my hands were shaking and my knees were wobbly.

Damn! How was I going to explain this expulsion, this failure to my editor? No editor would believe that I had only asked two straightforward reportorial questions to elicit her rage. It was going to be Vreeland's word against mine. A third party had not audited the interview. I was a rising journalism star in big, big trouble.

Quaking, I locked myself in a telephone booth and called my editor. I hated making that call. I hated being put in this despicable and embarrassing situation. I stammered out the short scenario. What I didn't know is that Vreeland had already telephoned my editor and complained. He said, at first facetiously, that I could extract the "out" from my description of being "thrown out" and that, in reality, I had the upper hand.

What?!!!!

He said I didn't need Vreeland to write about Vreeland's *Vogue*?!!!! He told me to editorialize my impressions, my ideas, my theories about Vreeland's new editorial stance. And, when I did, he syndicated my piece. It went national. It was a notable coup d'état.

I'm telling you this story because Big Red, as I named her, continued to be the untouchable tyrant strolling from glory to glory. I never expected to hear from Big Red again. But years later, when she was sanctified as the revered curator of The Metropolitan Museum's Costume Institute, her publicist telephoned me.

"Dee-ah-nah really wants to do an interview with you," she sang and I thought I heard sincerity in the underpinnings of her melodious voice. I believed her because when I told this publicist about my first encounter and subsequent editorial on Vreeland and *Vogue*, she knew all about the fiasco.

"Dee-ah-nah thought you were gutsy," she laughed. "Dee-ah-nah likes gutsy women."

This time the interview, my first and last, was in Vreeland's Manhattan apartment. Again we were surrounded by incense candles. She could live neither without that lingering scent nor without extravagant melodrama. We sat beneath a red paisley sheik-like tent strung from the center ceiling.

Big Red was a pitiful scarecrow version of her former self. She smelled sick. The inside gossip was that she was suffering from advanced colon cancer. She wanted to talk to me, set things straight, come full circle, make up for the lost interview.

We talked about a lot of things, especially pizzazz, a word she reportedly invented, and what it all boiled down to was: dare. She prized anything or anyone who dared to be different.

When I was being described as an original, I never thought of myself as being isolated or different. I just thought; "It's my job to be creative." Nothing scares me, not even originality.

When my kids were small, I took them to the zoo to see the gorillas. The zoo keeper was their best friend. We would go to his room, a very shabby box with great big chairs, and he'd release the gorillas from their cages and into the room the animals came. The gorillas sat in the chairs. The children sat in the gorillas' laps, resting comfortably. It was killing me, seeing my sons hugged by gorillas. But I controlled myself because I thought I was achieving an objective. I wanted the boys to learn to be afraid of nothing. Look: I didn't take the possibility of harm for granted. I am not a fool. But I feel, with great certainty, that my plan worked. My sons are not afraid. And if they are afraid, they don't discuss their fears. They conquer them quietly.

I love fashion. It's all because I was born in Paris. I was surrounded by fashion. To be fashionable, you just have great concentration. The center of concentration is your self-image. You have to wear clothes that you perceive to be a reflection of the way you feel about yourself. Notice I said "feel," rather than "see yourself." As I'm talking to you, I do not see me. You see me. Anyway, I've never really been fashionable. To be fashionable, you always have to be seen at the right place with the right people at the right time. I like to go where the grass is high and the streams bubble over rocks. That is not a fashionable setting. Or is it?

When I worked, I didn't have the slightest notion that I had power. I just thought I had a good job. Well, I'll tell you about retirement. It make you senile. My idea of a good day is having more work to do that you can possibly imagine.

You asked me before why I've always believed in exaggeration. Suddenly, it's come to me. I believe in going all the way. The extreme always comes out so well. You put everything into whatever it is you're doing. All your energy. Everything is cooking. The burners are up. I like that. Don't you?

There is a pause going on in the world now. The pause is about great luxury and great beauty. The world has become a little too lax about appreciation and care for great luxury and great beauty. Maybe that's why very few fashionable people are chic. Chic is a passé word. Today people are well-dressed, amusing, even picturesque. Chic requires people to look after their chicness. People who take care of you and your clothes and your environment. Chic has a lot to do with making what's natural look good, like pure silk or pure linen. Please don't ever ask me to discuss polyester.

My mother told me I was ugly. I didn't need to be told. I already knew. Children are very smart about things like that. I knew I wasn't pretty. But I wasn't hurt because I didn't care what people thought. I adored going to Russian dancing classes. The colors! The costumes! I concentrated on the beauty of the spectacle, not my lack of beauty. That's the way I've always been.

Women don't realize how easy it is to be a successful wife even if you have a career. You don't ever, ever mention your job to him. You see him only in the evening, so be charming. I had a fine husband. He never neglected me. I didn't even know what the word, neglect, meant. I was very spoiled.

I always live today for today. I never look back, except on pleasure. The other takes too much time. I prefer to look ahead.

I always see paths of opportunity. I've been thwarted and disappointed. But it never bothered me much. That's just the rhythm of life. And I've never permitted myself to be depressed. My dear, depression affects the liver.

I've never changed much in the sense of style. Change really has nothing to do with fashion. One's feelings change. One's reactions change. One learns to trust one's instinct, which changes with experiences. Your own lines of character go on forever with some adjustments. As for fashion, you just automatically lean to certain silhouettes.

I love red. Red is a cleansing color. Reds make other reds look wonderful. I rarely wear it now, because I don't see it. But if *you* wear red, I'm delighted, because I can see it. I do wear red nail polish even if it's passé. That's because I can see it.

I like to be alone but I also love audiences. I love the communication. People come to you out of the fog and say the most wonderful things. It's spooky.

I've always tried to give people something they've never thought of ... something new. And I've never underrated the public's intelligence and enthusiasm. I never heard the criticisms that I exaggerate my ideas too much. I work only one way: with all my vitality ... and I've always done what I bloody well please.

I've been known as a tough boss. Secretaries I interview have said to me: "I hear this is a busy job." And I've said: "What do you mean by busy?" The answer, in essence, has been: "It's busy all the time." Well, my answer is: "If this is not your kind of job, don't apply." On top of that, I expect perfection. What else is there? Perfection is everything. Of course I know I'm asking for a lot in this day and age where young ladies don't want to be busy.

Work is the greatest thing any of us do. I don't think about getting old except I'd like to be able to get along with less sleep. But, then, even as a young girl, when I was in boarding school, no one could get me up in the morning. And at three o'clock I was ready to take a nap. At no time in my life have I ever been able to say: "I'm an early morning person." I'm an evening person. And I've always done what I bloody well please, day or night.

Andrea Marcovicci

on developing a mindset

Andrea Marcovicci, who is no stranger to Carnegie Hall, is an old-fashioned torch singer in the cabaret style. She dons black velvet clothes that scream Lady, as opposed to the barely-there skimps of a Liberated woman, and when she props herself atop a grand piano, she is a classy dame singing old truths about man-woman love. Her repertoire covers the range of good, bad, and Mr. In-between relationships.

No one, not even Bobby Short, can musicalize a woman's innate sentimentality and vulnerability the way she can. She's marvelous, too marvelous for words, whether she's singing about love not being such a many-splendored thing or promising lyrically that wishing will make it so.

The New York critics, among the grumpiest in the world, gaze upon her work benignly. But, from time to time, Marcovicci has been under fire from feminists who've been vocal about her sentimental renderings, especially those that portray women as hapless and hopeless romantics.

Feminists want Marcovicci, and the whole world, to believe that modern women don't get into love matches that reduce them to schmaltzy, mushy, soppy, slushy characters. Is that so? Show me one feminist who hasn't been in love, for better or worse, and I'll show you a fibber. The world's a-changing, but some things never change. Love, in its glory or lack of glory, is still the same old story. Besides, as one

New York Times observer recently put it, Marcovicci "can turn a love song inside out."

I went to the Algonquin Hotel's famous Oak Room to talk to Marcovicci about these foolish things and how they affected her job, her life and her lifestyle. She has long been the Algonquin's answer to The Carlyle Hotel's Bobby Short (Café Carlyle). Although Bobby sings some of the same love songs, the feminists have, as far as I know, left him alone.

What we have here is a feminist, a woman making a name for herself singing about love, being faulted by some women who'd like us to believe that love is a 50-50 deal. Love has nothing to do with equality. The more love you give, the more love you get—or don't get. Love is a lottery, even in the feminist world.

The thrill is that Marcovicci continues to sing stories that spin around the complexities of being in love: loving the wrong man, love gone wrong, pining love, fleeting love, bleeding love, perfect love, rollicking love, lost love, romantic love, real love, and unrequited love. Feminists aren't exempt from any of the above.

It's not easy to make the molehill theory work when the mountain you face is feminism. I asked Marcovicci what fuels her ambition to get out there and sing her heart out despite the backlash? Marcovicci told me that to be ambitious means that you take the talent you were given as far as you can take it, and if you're happy in your work, that's all that matters. She boiled it down to two little words: "a mindset."

ﾠ Feminists are supposed to be beyond heartbreak. I have been asked to justify politically why I am singing torch songs. Gloria Steinem came to hear me sing. She has been a very big influence on me. I didn't want her to get the wrong idea, to think that I was propagating the old tradition of the woman who allows herself to be mistreated by a man and still loves him.

But that's the nature of a torch song. A feminist can get her heart broken too.

My definition of romance is belief in the curative powers of love. I radiate hopefulness about the possibility that love exists. Love is easier and closer than you might think it is. It could exist in a relationship you already have but don't recognize as love.

Many women pick the wrong men in their lives. It comes from illusions presented in the movies, songs and books—but especially the movies. You get a picture of perfect love in your head. He's handsome! He's strong! He's never going to be mean to you! Love is idealized. In a movie, they know where their noses go in a kiss. It's not a fumbling, embarrassing experience like it can be in real life.

Women ignore the sweet guys who are right under their noses. They say: "Ah, here's a friend." Maybe women should get smart and love the men who love them.

First you have to love yourself.

I'm a great believer in elegance. It adds to the beauty of life. If you're someone who really listens to people who talk to you, you're elegant. Kindness is elegance. Pursuing your own interests without hurting anyone is elegant. A really elegant person doesn't have airs.

I used to think that in order to get up and sing you had to have an "act" to justify your existence. I relied on written dialogue. Now I've learned to trust me. When you trust yourself, you tell the truth. And the truth is always interesting because there are no tricks involved.

There's a cathartic value to love songs. It's cheap therapy. People say about a lost romance: "Get over it!" But there's always a lot of pain left over. People come to hear me sing and they cry over their lost loves. In a way, crying is therapy.

I know what it is to be emotionally bankrupt. You feel a sense of momentary helplessness, a kind of cold fire inside. Your heart pounds.

When you're lost, it's good to imagine something you want to see—a panda, Venice, your mother's face. You need focus. It's how you get outside yourself, even in your greatest despair. A focus makes you realize that you've still got desires. A desire can cancel out despair.

When I first started singing, I was very self-conscious and nervous. I've grown up. I've given up false ideas of what I should be. I used to have a strong obsession about how I looked. I was one of the original anorexics. I wasted time worrying about how I dressed.

There were times in my life I considered myself a failure. Success, in the worldly sense, eluded me. In 1980, I gave up. It lasted one day. I said: "I've failed. I have to find another way to make a living."

I had huge notions of what I was going to be. I set time limits on myself. That was the trouble. Once I gave up my unrealistic notions of success—massive success—I began to accept things on a day-to-day level. My transformation started three years ago when I began to sing again.

I started to sing torch songs that I wanted to sing, not songs that I thought were going to make me famous. There's an enormous difference. I changed from being scared to someone who's confident. Amazingly, when I relaxed I became a real success. Failure is an important lesson. What you learn from failure is that it doesn't kill you. You don't die! People don't take chances because they're afraid of rejection. But you only hit what you dare to aim at.

Liv Ullmann

on coping with death

Mom used to say that life was like an outlaw, that it snuck up on you and, because you can't protect yourself from the unknown, you are its inevitable prey. I knew that. But she also believed that endings weren't The End unless you thought they were.

But once, when she started talking about the unpredictable twists and turns of everyday life, I got scared. I knew that jumbled in the general undercurrent of our conversation lay her desire to prepare me for her death, to cushion the blow. She talked like this before I knew that cancer was stalking her. She was amazingly nonchalant. Her words were gloomy. Her attitude wasn't. She was preparing her own emotional hospice and mine.

Toward the end, she also talked about "living deaths," a phrase she used to describe human relationships that still existed but had gone awry. She believed you had to make peace with lost loves or, she said, they haunt you forever. Always imagine, she said, that endings are the mark of beginnings—like a circle.

She wanted me to believe that walking alone, without her, was not only possible, it was expected. I pledged allegiance to the idea of coping, but it was only a silent understanding between us.

I wasn't at Mom's side at the moment the angels claimed her. But a few hours earlier, listening to her desperate gasps to breathe, I was angry that the ruling force of life and death, had put her, a good-good woman, in such a bad-bad situation.

I went home to a dark house. I kept it dark because it matched my heart. I looked out of the window and the bare branches of the November treescape looked like black lace against the dark sky. There was a lone star up there. I locked glances with it. I told it that Mom was hurting and I ordered it to release her from her pain. I told it to tell the ruler of the universe, the being that Mom had called "the man upstairs," that I was now willing to release her to a grander scheme about which I knew nothing.

I am telling you this story because in it is ensconced a miracle.

Mom's death and my prayer of permission to release her from my sphere, were simultaneous. I told God what to do and it was done. I had not issued a plea. I had bossed God around and God allowed it. The memory of this answered prayer is humbling. In the remaining recesses of the deepest cut of all, grieving for a loved one, there is the belief that, in some small way, I am a continuation of her. I am the circle she was talking about.

At about the time I began to accept the wisdom of Mom's other death theory—about taking the best from finished relationships and friendships—I met Liv Ullmann. The interview, though brief and precious, was on common ground. Ours was the universality of death experiences, a reality that leaves no one untouched. She shared with me her two major experiences with death: the death of her father and the death of her liaison with the international Swedish film director, Ingmar Bergman.

    ❧   I was five years old when my father died. My mother romanticized his death. She said: "Daddy is sitting in heaven looking down at you." I wrote him letters, begging him to come back.

My mother's way of dealing with death was wrong. She didn't face death, look it in the eye. She rewrote it. She didn't allow us to grieve. I think tears and suffering are a way of self-healing.

I also know the grief of leaving someone you love. Someone alive. Someone who is there but won't be there for you.

You can't always be strong and brave. You have to cope. But you can cope only when you question things. When you learn to live with difficulty, that's coping. When you go on despite the difficulty, that's coping. Sometimes, as you cope, you cry.

When I parted from Bergman I was in despair. But he left his phone open to me. We talked ten times a day. I went to Rome. Then, one day, sitting in the sun, I wrote him a good-bye letter. I said: "It's over between us."

Later, how we laughed about that. He had recognized it was over for us five months earlier. He just let me go through my sorrow until I came to my own realization.

We are friends. It was my relationship with him that advanced my sense of confidence. He said I was a good actress. He never told me what to do in a scene. He made me feel he trusted me, my judgment. He recognized my talent and he liked me as a person and a woman. That gave me my first deep sense of esteem.

Even lost love turned out good. Loves that didn't last became friendships.

The other day I sat with a friend and told her the things that trouble my life. She told me the things that trouble her life. We burst out laughing. They were the same troubles.

I wish people would talk more to each other about their alikeness.

We look at other people and think they're better off, more attractive, more secure. In reality, they aren't. What all people have in common is their wondering, their questioning, their curiosity, their fearfulness. If people would indulge in the art of conversation, they'd realize their commonalities.

The moment of failing is painful. You think people don't recognize your abilities. It hurts because you think you're not living up to your expectations. It's feeling that you're less than you really are.

But failure is temporary. It lasts only if it makes you better.

The way to get over failure is to try again. If you fail again, then you have to try again and again. I never give up. I have failures only I know about. I'm always trying to correct them.

I've never believed much in psychological therapy. I'm my best guide. I confront myself. I question what I do. I walk with myself. I trust my own instincts. If you're not an evil person, you should trust your gut reaction. This is the truth of you.

I used to think a husband was there to look after you. Now I realize that I'm not in a relationship in which I'm "the little woman." I'm not a housewife. And I don't feel guilty about that. Before, it troubled me.

Marriage is companionship and friendship with love. You feel somebody is on your side, somebody dependable. I'm also there for my husband [Donald L. Saunders], someone equally dependable. I'm more tolerant now. I no longer expect my husband to have the same interests as me. My new attitudes are born of past experiences.

I have learned from my mistakes.

Ann Jillian

on physical alterations

Ann Jillian is an entertainer, a very beautiful blond actress who'd been filming a miniseries when the doctors told her that a double mastectomy was immediately and absolutely necessary. Eleven days after Ann Jillian underwent the radical surgery, she went back to work. She even juggled the chemotherapy sessions with her filming schedule.

Those are the facts.

The reality was that the surgery weakened her and the chemotherapy made her nauseous. She threw up frequently—or, to quote her, "every seven minutes"—and she felt a sense of humiliation. The other reality was that she had a bodice of scars. Humiliated and depressed, she thought that her married love match to Andy Murcia, a former Chicago policeman, was doomed. She was in a state of emotional frenzy.

Jillian remembers her episode with cancer in two distinct, but interrelated, chapters.

One: Working up the courage to show her scar to her husband.

She delayed the moment of truth for one month. Her husband kept on insisting he wanted to see the scars. He told her he wanted her to get over her emotional fears, so that she would get on with her physical recovery. But Jillian was nagged by an overriding worry: would her husband think her body had taken an ugly turn? Would he love the scars like he had loved her breasts?

The other theme was her need to develop an overwhelming desire to do battle with cancer, to fight the "alien thing," as she called it. Slowly but surely, she adopted the attitude that although cancer had invaded her body it was not going to snatch the life from it.

"If one cancer cell got loose, if it was too small to be detected by hand or instrument, I am going to kill it," is the way she described how she was going to kill the killer.

I did not expect Andy Murcia to sit in on the interview. But he was there, as an observer, and he listened carefully to everything his gorgeous wife said about the most important thing that ever came between them.

When she spoke of the moment that she stripped and showed him her new self, they looked at each other and they were lost in each other's presence. The interview came to a halt. I left quietly, without saying good-bye. They never noticed. They had moved toward each other, caught in a gentle embrace of mutuality.

  I have a great love of life, and that's what has to overcome all your fears. If something like cancer is there, it won't disappear. Women have a fear of breast examination. They'd rather stay in ignorance than face the situation. If cancer is detected early enough, you can be cured.

  Sure, I thought of cancer as a major obstacle. Intellectually, I reasoned I was in a serious situation. I knew cancer could be fatal. First I tried to deal with how I was going to adjust to this lousy situation. But I also thought, "This lousy operation is going to save my life."

  I looked into my husband's eyes and I saw fear. I knew he was thinking, "This is it." I begged God not to let me die. That was my moment with God. I actually surrendered myself to my Creator.

  The surgery meant I was going to lose my breasts. Like any other woman in a similar situation, I wondered how it would affect our relationship. There was a tender moment between us then. Andy understood the loss I was feeling. Not just in theory. But for real.

There was a sense that I was being taken care of, as in the marriage commitment of "sickness and health." It was not just surface love. It didn't mean "I love you the way I saw you and the way I always want you to be." This was a remarkable revelation to me.

My husband tells me he had one thought: "Will Ann live?" After the operation, I found it difficult to reveal myself to Andy. I didn't allow him to see me for a month. The confrontation was delayed because I had this worry: "Will he really love me when he sees me physically altered?"

He wanted me to show him the scar. He wanted me to get over the emotional fears so I could get on with the physical recovery.

I showed myself to him and he said: "So, you've had a mastectomy and I'm still here." He hugged me. Then he said: "I'm not only still here. I'm not going anywhere."

He was persuasive and firm. I was relieved. People talk about my having strength. But my husband grasped the moment and led me.

Friendship is the basis of a good marriage. My husband and I are best friends. We're not always in tandem but we respect each other's opinions. We're both feisty individuals. But we both have heart, especially for each other.

If there ever was a time we were one, this was it. We cried together as one. It wasn't joy as we know joy but I had a gut feeling that I was understood. I felt, in the true sense, that we belonged to one another. Each of us knew what "I love you" meant.

Jackie Collins

on doing anything

She's loquacious and vibrant, a lovely woman with a slow-motion smile and mischievous eyes. She wears her hair in a classic Holly-wood-inspired lion's mane, wears diamonds the size of bird's eggs and is famous for being what critics call the world's flash-and-trash queen.

But, truly, her flash isn't trash. Her name is Jackie Collins and she, even more than her sister, actress Joan Collins, is dressed to thrill. It's relatively easy. She lives in the shadow of Rodeo Drive, in Los Angeles, boutique heaven to the rich and famous. She loves all the jazz. Her clothes are couturier and her sparkling diamonds are real, by golly. She writes steamy best-sellers with titles that are as theatrical as she is: *Hollywood Wives*, *The Stud*, *Lucky*, and, of course, the classic of all times, *The Bitch*.

What's terrific about London-born Collins is that she, an expert on Hollywood bitch information, isn't a bitch herself.

She's blunt, ambitious and funny. She's honest too. She'll tell you straight out that she had a fling with Marlon Brando, later married "a Jewish prince" and, after a divorce, got "into drugs." She'll also tell you that when she had two daughters (now adults) with London business-man Oscar Lerman, "mummy" wasn't the first baby babble she taught them. "Anything." That was their first utterance, as in you-can-do-anything.

She told them that so often that they mimicked her instantly. It got to the point where she, the mummy who'd done practically every-thing, would simply look at her girl babies and they'd say with inno-cent conviction: "Anything!"

There's another thing she'd like you to understand: her politics are feminist but those who reign in the movement probably don't regard her as a card-carrying member.

Ask why. She'll tell you.

Do you think for a second that she, Jackie Collins, would ever scrape off her make-up and pin her long hair into a bun? Nope. Does Jackie Collins have hairy legs? Nope. Do you think she'd give up smudging her eyelids and ringing them like Cleopatra? Nope. Get it? Yup. Collins will do anything she wants, including her pursuit of glam-our. If the militants don't like it, too bad.

Her racy-lacy lingerie, obviously too couture to be Victoria's Se-cret, barely disguises the décolletage peeking from her tailored suit jacket. "I'm not a bra burner," Collins says suddenly and unnecessarily.

Jackie Collins was thirteen when she began her anything odyssey. It continues, gaining momentum, and that's the way she wants it.

My father was always a stern man. Growing up, I was fright-ened of him. He's shocked by my books. He won't read them. I couldn't care less. He wouldn't understand them anyway. He has no idea how far women have progressed. I don't expect approval from him. I have to approve of myself.

When I was a small girl and I asked him a question, he'd say: "You're old enough and ugly enough to know." The word "ugly" was demeaning. But that's what made me want to suc-ceed. I had to prove I wasn't ugly and that I could do anything that I set my mind to do.

When I was thirteen, I seized control of my life. I simply refused to go to school. I played truant. I went to the movies. I forged notes. When I was fifteen, I was thrown out of school, expelled. I've made it without an education. Actually, I'm an eccentric.

I was a woman alone in Hollywood at age fifteen. Men

were always making obligatory passes. I was literally chased around the desks of movie directors and producers. I ran fast. As I was running, I said to one man: "But what about your wife?" And as he chased me, he said: "My wife is different." That man didn't catch me. No man ever caught me unless I wanted to be caught. I have self-confidence and self-respect.

Even ugly women can create an aura if they project an air of belief in themselves.

Unintelligent men think women should be eternally twenty-two, blonde, have big boobs and no brains. That's their concept of the ideal woman. I have my concept of the ideal woman. She should live her life the way the single man always lived his life. Sexually, she should be free. If she meets a man and wants to go to bed, she should. If she meets a man and feels like saying, "Don't call me, I'll call you," she should.

A woman should not get married until she has experienced life, especially life with men. You should never get married and find yourself asking: "What have I missed?"

I'm a feminist. I'm not sure the feminist movement acknowledges me. I'm not a feminist who scrapes off her make-up and pins back her hair. I'm not a bra-burner. If a man said, "Let's burn our jockstraps," he'd be laughed out of existence.

I make more money now than my husband. I regard that money as mine. But I use it as ours. My husband is a secure man. He doesn't encroach on my career, yet he is always looking after me. He watches my accountant. I feel this is our success ... my husband is incredibly supportive. But he's in control of his life, not mine. We have an equal relationship. He doesn't tell me what to do. I don't tell him what to do. That's the secret of a good marriage, creating the feeling that no one belongs to anybody.

The Hollywood wives would have loved to see me fail. They were jealous that I could make more money than their men. They have to get money through their men and that really galls them. I ignore these women. No. I laugh at them.

I have a few wonderful female friends (in Hollywood), but these friendships have been carefully tested.

I write about the world I know: Hollywood. Hollywood is sleaze city. In Hollywood, if you're caught cheating, you "fail up." What I mean is that somebody else will give you a job at the top of another company. It's the old-pals act. Women cannot "fail-up." If they fail, they fail. If a woman director has a movie flop, she will never work again. I've seen this happen frequently.

Yet Hollywood is an interesting world. The typical Hollywood wife gets up in the morning and, first thing, checks her nails. If a nail is broken, her day is ruined. She telephones her manicurist immediately to come and fix it, fast. Then she has her legs waxed. Then the exercise specialist comes to her home to help her streamline her body. Then she goes to lunch with a friend, someone with whom she can trash everybody and find out who's doing the best plastic surgery. Then she gets her hair combed, goes home to get ready for a party, and her husband arrives from the office. He feels amorous. But she says: "No, no, no. I just got my hair done." That, you know, is why many Hollywood marriages fail.

Being a good-looking woman in Hollywood is difficult. Men are scared off by beautiful, talented women. They feel threatened. There's the chance the woman might do their job better. It's called chauvinism. My father is a terrific chauvinist. He always was. Whenever we had roast beef, he always got the best cut. He thought it was his due. I thought it was unfair.

I plan to live until I'm eighty-five. I will continue to be eccentric. Canny, too. I'll invite all my relatives in, videotape them secretly, study the tapes and figure out which ones want all my money. Then I'll give it all to the one who doesn't want anything.

Barbara Taylor Bradford
& Susan Isaacs

on trying a little fearlessness

Rarely, if ever, do two famous women tell you, separately and in totally unrelated interviews, the same basic story of the gutsy inner searching that it took to banish their self-doubt and fuel their idled creative machinery.

Rarely, if ever, would the two famous women, who happen to be major literary stars, make it clear that to release and energize the power of their imagination, they had to unlock a door they had unwittingly closed on themselves.

Their commonality is linked to the commonality of talented women everywhere, who know, deep down, that they "have it," but they think they can't possibly "make it," so they put themselves "on hold."

Although each woman was, and is, in a different situation, hails from a different geography and a different background, each described herself to me as "ordinary." They were different but so alike in their self-appraisals. As each interview escalated, as the impetus of their desire to excel became more tightly focused, the word ordinary stretched into the phrase, "ordinary housewife."

But I wasn't interviewing ordinary women. They only thought they were ordinary when, in fact, they were being interviewed because they are extraordinarily accomplished.

I reminded each woman of that. And I asked each woman the same question: How, in fact, did you switch from commonplace thinking to adopting an attitude of can-do and will-do? The key, each said, had been staring them in the face: when you are fearful, try a little fearlessness.

I would like you to meet two famous self-made millionaires: Barbara Taylor Bradford and Susan Isaacs. They're totally unlike physically. But, emotionally and professionally, they're mirror images of each other.

London-born Bradford, a glamorous blonde whose long hair is a sleek pageboy, leans toward any color that is vanilla. Isaacs is a handsome brunette with a big frizzy hairdo and a penchant for dark lipstick and black anything. Bradford's first novel, A *Woman of Substance*, sold 12 million copies and was made into an Emmy-nominated television miniseries. Brooklyn-born Isaacs's best-seller, *Compromising Positions*, was made into a movie. Both continue to be publishing superstars.

Even they might not even know two other parallels that speak reams. They both work at home. And each woman began her career working in a relatively unimportant office position and moved up quickly. Bradford dropped out of school at sixteen to be a cub reporter for the *Yorkshire Evening Post*. At eighteen she was an editor. Isaacs dropped out of Queens College to work in an office at *Seventeen* magazine and quickly became a senior editor.

But to explode on the literary scene as popular phenomenons, each woman had to possess the best of herself. It took a little courage. They were both frightened.

Barbara Taylor Bradford

    I started four novels that I never finished.

I was super critical of myself. I never thought I was good enough. I was also afraid of failing. That was a very big thing for me to get over. So I found all sorts of excuses not to continue, not to finish any of the novels I had started. Subconsciously I thought: "If I finish one, if I send it to an agent, maybe no one will publish it." Rejection and failure were, to me, synonymous. I thought: "I probably won't make it as a novelist." So I started four books, for heaven's sake. I was just playing games with myself.

On a Monday, sitting at home, I talked to myself. "I don't like what I'm doing." "What do you want?" "I want to write about a strong woman who makes it in a man's world." "That's not interesting." "Why?" "Women today are doing that all the time." "Well, why don't you go back in time? Why don't you write about a strong woman who makes it in a man's world when such things were impossible?"

Then a phrase ran through my head. I heard myself say to myself, "Write about a woman of substance." I wrote the phrase down. I looked at it. "That's it!" I said. By the end of the day, I had an outline for the book. Deep in my bones, I knew I would finish that manuscript.

My mood switched from fear of failure to self-confidence. I had read a phrase somewhere that "character is plot." That phrase came to mind and I knew instantly in my heart and in my head what that meant. The character of the character provides the plot. Don't you see? I'm the author of my life because of my character, the type of person I am. Real people create their own plot, their own lives. Fictional people do the same. Once I understood that, I tackled the idea that I could be a novelist.

That Monday I told you I hit upon the idea for A Woman of Substance, I saw myself clearly. Between 1971 and 1975, I was merely practicing writing fiction. I was doing my exercises, preparing myself to be a serious novelist. Those five years were my initiation. Once I understood that, I was on my way.

I've always admired strong women, survivors. The spirit of survival is not being dominated by anything or anybody. A survivor is independent of thought and feeling, regardless of the price. I never needed to join a group to feel emancipated.

Strength was an aptitude pounded into me by my mother.

She was a housewife, a nurse, a nanny. She was determined and indomitable. When she was a baby, her father died. When she was fourteen, her mother died. An aunt immediately sent her to a hospital, to be a student nurse. My mother had a great sense of loss, but she carried on.

She married my father who had an artificial leg. My brother died as a baby, of meningitis. When the Depression hit, my father was out of work. My mother supported us. My mother is the best part of me. Her strength continues to pervade my life. She was a good woman, saintly, and every day she told me this: "I love you. You are the best. You are the brightest. You are the most beautiful. You are the most talented." When I did what I thought was my best, she told me I could do more. When I asked her what she meant by "best," she said: "Best is going beyond what you think is your best, beyond what is expected." My mother was talking about an attitude, a stance, not being a crybaby. These are the kind of women who attract my curiosity and imagination. I am compelled to write about them.

Success is having your pride satisfied. Once a friend asked me if I minded being "a popular novelist." I said: "I sure as hell wouldn't want to be an unpopular novelist." Commercial success isn't necessarily bad. I have readers. That's my achievement. That's my success.

Look, this is the truth. I wasn't the most beautiful or the most talented. My mother expected me to be those things, so I took great care with myself. I was always carefully groomed. I worked hard. I took advantage of opportunities.

The day my mother died, I found her diary tucked away in a desk. I opened it. On the date I first left home to go to work in London, I saw there, in her handwriting, this entry: "Barbara went to work today. All the sunshine has gone out of my life." She let me sail forth into the world, urging me on, insisting on excellence. She knew that a child is only lent to you. So she let me go. It was a terrible day when I read that entry.

I realized how much I really meant to her. But she left me the greatest legacy a mother can give a daughter, the desire to excel.

Susan Isaacs

My heroines are always audacious. Women who succeed have to be audacious. It's not that they've taken assertiveness training courses. The truth is that most people lack confidence, trip over their own feet. The person who succeeds says: "I'm scared! I'm going to throw up! Oh well, if I throw up, I'll clean it up and go on." Now that's audaciousness.

Audacious people take chances. I know what it is to take chances.

I wanted to write a novel. But I said to myself: "Who am I to write a novel?" I could write a simple declarative sentence. But I was a housewife, a suburban middle-class Jew. I had enormous self-doubts. I wasn't Virginia Woolf. I wasn't Jacqueline Susann.

It took me a year to get up the courage to write. That whole year, I did the silliest things to avoid writing. Like, I spent hours in a department store choosing socks for my son. He was six. Do you think he cared about socks? And I hated myself. I had a strong urge to write. But I was too fearful.

One day, when I was profoundly unhappy and miserable, I ordered a book on how to write a novel. Now let me tell you something. Nobody can tell you how to write. But the book came—it stipulated simple, manageable requirements. Like, list your characters. Like, create a plot.

Suddenly, within seven or eight hours, I had written a plot for my first book. It was an exhilarating release. I thought: "I don't have an insane, grandiose ambition. What I've got is the start of a book."

Real success is hard to achieve. You have to create some-thing worthwhile, something of value. It's a feeling of achievement. I know when I've written something good. I read it and say: "Hot damn!"

I don't have a glitzy life. Writing is not a glitzy business. Writing is the adult equivalent of sitting alone in a room, sucking your thumb and daydreaming. The main difference is that the daydreaming is structured and you get paid. The basis of the whole exercise is that you have a desire to tell a story.

I work at home. Now that's pressure. I'm always there for the plumber. My kid has a temperature of 103 degrees. I'm there. The dog might throw up on the rug. The butcher may call to ask how I think I want the veal cutlets sliced.

Home is my job. I don't work elsewhere because I'm in charge of the house as well as in charge of the writing. When you work at home, you stare into a word processor, a glowing green thing. But you're creating an alternate world on the screen.

Catherine Deneuve

on being a mother

French actress Catherine Deneuve is often described in sweeping paradoxes. When told she has been called a woman of "lustful purity," or "enigmatic eroticism," she bursts into laughter.

She seems to be as ephemeral as whipped cream but, in the extreme close-up of an interview, she is as icy and distant as that famous sculpture of her as Marianne, the personification of the French Republic that has graced its 36,394 Town Halls.

What adds a patina of mystery and dimension to her beauty is that she looks vulnerable but is, in fact, a woman who is governed by her own whimsy. Sometimes she blows hot. Sometimes she blows cold. One minute she is smiling benignly. Her next glance is withering. Above all, she values her independence. She acts accordingly. Without fail.

And there we were, taking tea at Boston's Four Seasons Hotel.

She smelled good, like an expensive bouquet of spring flowers. She looked good in her impeccable Yves Saint Laurent suit. I had been warned by her publicist that Deneuve would remain in a good mood only if I stuck to the subject of her choice: what constitutes beauty. That seemed reasonable. I was talking to an expert. Besides, the excuse for our meeting was strictly commercial. Deneuve was pushing a new $165-an-ounce perfume aptly named, Deneuve.

It never occurred to me to ask her about life in the mommy track.

She brought it up. Deneuve had children out of wedlock. One son with Roger Vadim. One daughter with Marcello Mastroianni. Cuddling a wailing baby, changing diapers or pushing a stroller along the Champs-Elysées seemed alien to her style.

But we got on the subject of the price of success, just how much a woman has to sacrifice to have, to hold and to sustain a career which, in her case, is on the international level. Deneuve grabbed at the word, *sacrifice*, and applied it to her view of modern motherhood. "I'm against sacrificing everything for motherhood," she said. Deneuve, who has always been the perfect example of femininity, didn't need to identify herself as a feminist.

I asked her to define motherhood. She called it "a heavy task." I reminded her that she was rich and that surely she had hired nannies to look after her babies. She saw dollar signs in my eyes. That's not the point, she objected. I saw the flash of exclamation marks in her eyes. Deneuve argued that mothers can be mothers and not cave into the demands of being mothers. She said that just because a woman gives birth does not mean that she must relinquish her independence, her career, her ambition, her looks.

Surprisingly, this turned out to be an issue with her.

Deneuve didn't speak at length about being a mother. She chose her words carefully, wisely, succinctly. Even her conversational shorthand made a point.

Deneuve is a mother. But, first, she is Deneuve. And Deneuve has many aspects.

~ Children are selfish. They complain a lot. But they'll never hear from me that I made great sacrifices for them. They'll never hear that I went through horrible divorces and stayed with them. One way or the other, children pay for so-called "sacrifices." My children know that I've led the kind of life I've wanted to lead.

I love my children. But sometimes motherhood is a heavy task. I work. I'm not there for them all the time. When I'm away, I'm away. When I'm there, I'm there. I'm against sacrificing everything for motherhood. It takes time for a woman to say "no" to her children's demands and not feel guilty. It's taken me over twenty years of practice not to feel guilty.

Women, by nature, are emotional creatures. Women put love into anything and everything they do. Love can be friendship. Love can be desire. Whatever, it's always emotional. Very few people can talk about their emotions because they are so deep, so personal.

I am often perceived as a contradiction. I have been described as a blend of sweetness and sophistication. It's a description I like. It's neither black nor white. It implies unpredictability. I can be civil or uncivil. I can be pleasant or unpleasant. I'm human. I'm certainly not in a good mood all the time.

When you work publicly, people think you should always be rested, pretty, nice and well-dressed. I don't always wake up in that kind of mood. So I say to myself: "Compose yourself." I compose myself a lot.

But when I think of my real image, I don't see it completed. In total, I see myself in bits and pieces. I see myself as a puzzle. I've never put the pieces together. Who is ever one person all the time?

I always think I could do more, be better. I'm pessimistic in a positive way. I'm never really totally satisfied with my films. I enjoy doing things more than seeing the results. Sometimes I get frustrated because I cannot control the finished product, the film itself. But I know that movie making is based on teamwork and that acting, itself, becomes abstract work. Still, I can do my best and not be shown doing my best.

Life is short. I think you've got to make life as interesting as possible. I like change. Two summers ago, I had short reddish hair. No one remembers that. They only remember my long blond hair.

Women think changing the color of their hair can change the tenor of their lives. They think they'll feel better, different, by being suddenly blond. But the glow doesn't last.

I've never gotten used to being called a sex symbol. It's not in my personality. I'm too serious. You can be voted good looking. But sexy is so much more precise. I often see large projections of myself on screen. I'm used to seeing myself as someone else, the character I play.

To feel "different," you've got to decide to be different. That all starts inside with your feelings about yourself. Men are trained to be tough, to repress their feelings. It's really very nice to have been born a woman.

Nora Ephron

on betrayal

Nora Ephron was in a snit. When it comes to the final memories of life with her ex-husband, Watergate reporter Carl Bernstein, she'll probably always be in a snit. Who can blame her? When she was seven months pregnant, she discovered that Bernstein was having an affair, reportedly with Mrs. Peter Jay, the wife of a former British Ambassador to the United States and the daughter of ex-Prime Minister James Callaghan.

She was sure she would go mad, as in crazy. But she was just plain mad, as in angry. Anger, when channeled, is an impetus.

After the baby came, Ephron wrote a novel, *Heartburn,* a thinly-veiled account of her outrage and reaction to her philandering husband. The comic memoir, later made into a movie starring Meryl Streep as Nora and Jack Nicholson as Carl, seemed like a kind of catharsis, a witty exorcism.

The question has always been whether or not Ephron authored the book as public way of getting back at Bernstein? When asked if, in fact, the book wasn't the perfect example of the ultimate revenge, she pretends to be both amused and shocked.

"Revenge?" she says, eyes widening in mock surprise. "I'd be Pollyanna-ish to say it didn't cross my mind."

When she was at Wellesley College, she penned hilarious accounts of life on campus and mailed them as letters to her parents, the successful Hollywood screenwriting team, Phoebe and Henry Ephron. Her mother telephoned her with excellent advice. "Everything is copy," her mother said. "You're a reporter. Take notes." Mostly she took notes on herself and invariably related certain crises to her own shortcomings. She's always said part of her trouble was having small breasts.

It would have been difficult, if not impossible, for Ephron to write *Heartburn* with such elegant wit if she hadn't been able to ease the pain of her betrayal with a sense of humor.

But it wasn't only her comedic streak that saw her through. It was her innate ability to break down the breakdown of her marriage into tiny little details, examine them through the microscope of herself and, detail by detail, put the experience of marital betrayal behind her.

Getting past an obstacle doesn't mean the obstacle is obsolete. It's always there. But Ephron could not cope with the resurfacing of this bad old memory if she hadn't come to grips with it.

I asked her how she did it. She spelled it out. Detail by detail.

When you are betrayed, your honest-to-God feelings are fury, hurt, and anger. One of the worst feelings that comes next is: "Can I do something?" You think: "I'll make his favorite dinner." Or: "I'll get a new haircut." Or: "I'll buy a fantastically beautiful dress." Or: "I'll read up on the economy." The whole idea is: "I'll get him back."

Some women never get beyond the point of accepting there is nothing they can do to get the man back. They spend their lives thinking they are capable of making the man love them again. I got over the "I-can-do-something" feeling. It took several weeks.

I've seen so many people, men and women, whose marriage ended melodramatically and who bore the wounds for years. Forever. It's all right to feel bad. But to go on bleeding? No. Anyway, I don't believe that there's only one person for anyone.

Acknowledging betrayal is the most awful emotion short of true disaster, like death. But betrayal is also one of the most interesting things you can go through. Betrayal is fascinating. You don't want to pretend it didn't happen. But when my marriage ended, the last thing I wanted people to think is that I was squashed flat, wallowing in self-pity, defenseless, powerless, vulnerable in a hopelessly wounded way.

A lot of women are too happy being victims. It ties in perfectly with the worst things we learn about being women, namely: "whither thou goest, I go." And there's a secret kick to being a betrayed woman. When betrayed, you are immediately absolved of other major sins, like sloth or gluttony. Or middle sins, like jealousy and leaving crumbs in bed. The feeling of being a victim is comfortable, like being plunged in a warm bath.

To give up that feeling is a major move. You have to accept responsibility for your own life. You have to stop blaming whoever you're blaming. But there's a kind of freedom in deciding to do what you have to do. You feel great.

I had a good therapist and a lot of good friends. The friends let me know I was not alone. The therapist, a female, got me in touch with my self-destructive feelings, like guilt. A lot of women feel ashamed in finding themselves betrayed. You think you've done something you shouldn't have done. You think he has chosen someone over you. I cried during those sessions. Oh, I certainly cried. But it's an electrifying moment when you decide you're not sitting on someone's string, being jerked back and forth.

The moment you break with someone who's already broken with you, that's another satisfying moment. The initial truth is that he rejected you. But you were the one who said good-bye. In a bizarre way, you are the one who says the *real* good-bye. You can always say to yourself: "Well, I'm the one who walked out, the one who split." At least you can reactivate your ego. You, at least, have the illusion of your own worthiness, your attractiveness. And the pain lessens.

Divorce is idiotically painful. But a lot of things happened to me when my marriage ended. To find you are as strong as you turn out to be, that is an exhilarating experience. Despite the nightmare reality of being truly alone, you find you can handle it. It's a very odd high.

There are no terrible mistakes. Only mistakes. You make mistakes and you live through them and you turn them into something terrific. The point is: Do you want to? The moment you decide not to be passive about mistakes, when you make up your mind to do something about your mistakes, that's the turning point.

I never was a slouch. But you don't know how strong you are until your strength is tested. When you go through pain and come out okay, you develop a new confidence.

It's all so ludicrous, so funny. Given what we see every day. We think about betrayal as an occasional thing. We think we've been singled out. But half the world is being betrayed by the other half. We've also grown up with notions of the possibility of a romantic marriage. Despite the statistic to the contrary, we dream.

Sandra Bernhard

on compatibility

Comedienne and actress Sandra Bernhard, a glossy icon of pop culture, is definitely not what she seems to be. In person there is no brazen sneer. She's not at all contemptuous or sarcastic. All that bawdy drop-dead sophistication of her public image, from her simmering strut to her big-mouth shockers, is just surface glitz.

The real Bernhard is a complicated riddle, a woman who has had bouts with depression that lasted too long, with specific fears that include being haunted by imagined transportation disasters and, that old standard, being lonely in a crowd. One of her worst traumas is contracting herpes from a man she was with only once. A mist freezes in her penetrating glance when she says that if she saw "the creep" in a police lineup today, she wouldn't be able to identify him.

She broods openly about past indiscretions, but always in the clarity of hindsight. Without embarrassment, she tells you that therapy has helped her sassy-brassy professional self become compatible with her fearful-tearful personal self.

If there's one thing she wants in life, and out of life, it's compatibility. What she thinks of as a pot of gold at the end of the rainbow is staring her in the face. An interview is all about compatibility, a sharing of ideas and impressions, of making a connection. Our interview screamed compatibility. But she didn't see or hear herself that way I heard and saw her. I pinned her down. I asked her to define her concept of compatibility.

Bernhard, a doctor's daughter, was born in Flint, Michigan and grew up in Scottsdale, Arizona. She graduated from high school and worked as a Beverly Hills manicurist for five years.

She'd like to meet a man who'd view her as a congenial companion. Always. She'd like to go to a party and feel a sense of congeniality with the other partygoers. Always. She'd like to go onstage, on television, on camera and know for certain that her huge audience finds her antics most agreeable. Always.

Finally it dawned on me.

What made Bernhard's desire for compatibility so insatiable is that she wanted it constantly, whether she had an audience of one or an audience of millions. What she wanted was heaven on earth. Funny I should mention that, she said, and her smile was sad. We had come to the crux of an issue of her life: the clash of her expectations against the twist-and-turns of reality.

Compatibility, like all states of the human condition, is like a see-saw. It has its ups and downs. Surely we wouldn't be talking so intensely, so personally, if she hadn't learned how to resolve the conflicts of her divided self. What was her secret? She boiled it down. Her new mindscape, an intellectual exercise in-progress, was to neutralize incompatibilities by not blaming herself for situations that were out of her control. Bernhard then traced her trek from who she was to who she is.

    You don't know what a plunging V-neck depression is? It's a woman in a fabulous décolletage dress having a perfectly awful time at a sophisticated party.

That has happened to me. I'd look around and say: "What am I doing here? What's this all about?" Sometimes I'd go to a party out of curiosity. I'd people-watch. Then I'd say to the hostess. "Thanks. I'm leaving now." Then I'd flee.

It is this kind of situation that has made me aware of other people's sensitivities. It points out how alienated we are from each other, isolated. Now I surround myself with people with whom I don't have to pretend. At a cocktail party, wearing a low-cut dress, I'd have to put on an act.

Connections are very important to me. Once, I said I wanted to be worshipped. I was just kidding. I just want an audience who respects me. I want to continue to make connections. I've been in therapy. I used to think therapy had to do with being neurotic. It's not that. Talking to a therapist is learning how to be good to yourself. I'm entitled to that. I used to have a fear of being alone. I can now do things by myself. Once you're victorious over yourself, you enjoy life more.

My father studied hypnosis on records. When I was in the fourth grade, he made my hives disappear. He experimented on me. He told me my arms were like limp dishrags. He made me believe he could work magic on me. He cured my hives.

My father made a connection with me. I was pleased he was paying rapt attention to me. Now, if an audience doesn't pay attention to me, it's an alienating experience. I have to "get them." I have to make a connection. A connection is a triumph.

When I was in high school I thought I had valid ideas. But no one seemed to be listening. I wasn't a pretty, accessible blonde. Socially, I felt outside the norm. So I made my humor work. People paid attention to me when I was funny. Humor became my safety valve. It was a comfortable place to be. I discovered you could say intelligent, sharp things with humor and not appear didactic.

One of my childhood fears was that my mother was going to go blind from staring at an eclipse of the sun while I was away at camp. I still have fears, disaster fears. Whenever someone I love is flying somewhere, I listen to the news all day expecting to hear about the crash of that plane. I have fantasies about airport disasters and boating disasters and car disasters. Life is fragile. People disappear from situations that are out of their hands.

Sensitive people think about death because they're so aware of life. Yet when I indulge in fantasies, I have bursts of thought.

Out of these thoughts come ideas. Out of ideas come my work.

I'm a blithe spirit. I'm open to all kinds of experiences, especially on a romantic level. I've been hurt romantically. A blithe spirit takes a chance, for better or worse.

I have herpes. That's not a joke. It's an exhausting thing. You're ready to lose your mind. But I'm not embarrassed by it. It's a reality. I'm careful. I don't give it to my partners. I was with the guy once. He was a creep. If I saw him in a police lineup, I wouldn't know him. Now that's irony.

In my twenties, I flung myself into any situation. Now I'm a blithe spirit with discretion.

It used to be that I couldn't handle it when someone said he loved me. I've changed. I've allowed good people to come into my life and be generous on an emotional level. It used to be I was involved with people who were flawed. I had the upper hand. I was going to make them less flawed.

I've discovered you can't change people. If you try, what you lose is part of yourself. I used to be too hard on myself. But I've come to accept myself, my imperfections. I no longer look for someone to fill my expectations. I now look for someone with whom I can share my life, as is.

I used to have a fear of being alone. I can now do things by myself. Once you're victorious over yourself, you enjoy life more. Now I've proven myself. I've developed an audience who came to see me. The club owners don't have to provide an audience for me anymore. That's the best part of celebrity.

The darker side of me has fits and broods. I think about life's ultimate negatives. But one thing is different about me now: I'm quick to filter out the hurts that are beyond my control.

I'm always longing to be the best version of myself. Striving for the best is a constant state. You have to challenge yourself, open up to the next level of experience.

Candice Bergen

on living life to the fullest

Candice Bergen seems to have everything. Beauty. A fine acting career. A privileged lifestyle. But to have everything is not the same as having everything you want.

Candice had not been as close to her father as she had wished. They were at cross purposes. She resented his cool demeanor. She took it as a deficiency in their relationship. His distance bred a streak of hard-to-discard rebellion in her personality.

That used to be a problem.

When she wanted to get her father's undivided attention, she startled him into acknowledging her presence. For example, she flunked out of the University of Pennsylvania.

He wasn't happy about her academic failure. There was madness in her method. It worked.

They engaged in heated dialogue. That was better than nothing, which was fine.

Candice, who's as candid as the photographer's camera she once carried, traces the root of her early mutinies to Charlie McCarthy, the dummy to whom her late father, ventriloquist Edgar Bergen, was utterly devoted. Candice, in fact, had always thought of Charlie as a sibling rival. Later, when she got a little older and little wiser, she proved she was no dummy when she decided to impress her father by upstaging The Dummy in positive ways.

Her father was taken aback, totally surprised, when she nonchalantly staged a string of rapid successes as a model, a writer, a photographer, an actress. Her successes soothed her injured pride. But success is success. It isn't a substitute for paternal love. Nothing is.

When her father died, Candice retreated and she rethought their separate lives and their life together. She became more and more aware that the careful use of one's time and one's decision are important.

Without sounding maudlin, and with a twinkle in her eye, Candice even pondered her own death and disposal. "Will it be a burial or a burning?" She asked the rhetorical question of herself. I did not ask it of her. Beginning to sound like Murphy Brown, she said the answer was still under consideration. She was too busy living life to the hilt.

What she had decided was to revamp and upgrade her old rebellion, fine-tune it, ground it, purify it, set it to new standards, make it more idealistic. When we talked, she was in the midst of changing her style from I'm-going-to-show-you to I'm-going-to-show-myself.

This self-power attitude took on new significance when, as this book went to press, legendary producer Don Hewitt tapped Bergen to contribute to his new, expanded 60 Minutes. Bergen could go from the fictional journalist to a real one.

It's no wonder that now she rebels against wasting precious time, at not focusing her best energy and drive on the projects and people that matter in her life. She rebels against taking her own gifts for granted, at not stretching her talents to the maximum.

    I never thought I had much courage. Maybe I've just had counter-phobia. I force myself to do things I'm frightened of doing. For a lot of years, I didn't take risks. Then I realized that taking risks is the point of living. It's what makes you grow.

I never wanted my beauty to matter. It always makes me nervous to think it makes a difference to other people. When you lose your looks, what do you do? Disappear? I've tried to make my looks irrelevant. Not in the movies, of course. I mean in my everyday life. I was supposed to be at Gloria

Steinem's recent fiftieth birthday party. Women like Gloria remind other women how great they can look at fifty. Women don't have to go onto an ice floe and die when they turn forty. Look at Raquel Welch. Look at Jane Fonda. When I do, I say to myself: "Hey, wait a minute." That is not to say I don't hate places like Beverly Hills where you see so many faces that have had so many facelifts that the women can't smile or eat. They have to take their food through a straw.

I've had a fairy-tale life with a dark underside. But everyone's childhood has a dark underside. There's not a child who ever had enough love, who didn't wish he or she didn't have a brother or sister. My childhood had an eccentric side. You know, dummies and magic. But maybe that was also part of the fairy-tale side. I know that in a lot of ways my childhood was enchanted.

But I wish I had been more connected to my father and mother. I wish the love we felt for each other had been expressed. If I had to do it over again, I'd be more open with my affections. I also know that my parents worked hard to give me a sense of values in Hollywood. The kids I grew up with were smothered in excess. My parents refused to give in to that. And that's what saved my neck.

And now I want everything I do to count. I'm very conscious of time passing. There's not an infinite amount of time left and I can't squander minutes or places or situations. In your youth, you can be forgiven that. But not anymore. Do days pass more slowly if you don't work? Does time pass more slowly if you're in the country? Does it mean the happier you are, the more quickly time passes? I've felt like a geezer just inching along. Then, recently, I realized that a person I considered a "new" friend was someone I had met ten years ago.

I always hope I'll be an exception to dying. I've actually thought a good deal about dying. I'm obsessed by it. Since I was fourteen, I've wondered what would happen to my body when I die. I've never wanted to be buried because I'm claustrophobic. Cremation almost seemed violent to me. I've thought maybe it would be preferable to be blown up by a land mine, camera in hand.

I know this about death: too many people die when they're not supposed to. People die just when their lives seem to peak. Now when I look at death, I look at life. The sooner you're aware of death, the sooner you make the most of life. It's what gives you a healthy sense of urgency. Now I live life as fully and openly as I can with the people I truly care about.

I'm not driven. I used to perceive ambition somewhat as a dirty word. Maybe ambition has been given a bad rap. People who have been singled out to personify ambition seem to be monstrous. Ambition, at its most positive, is a commitment and passion to what you do. That's the good side of ambition. Women have not been conditioned to be ambitious. In the Walt Disney world of things, women were expected to grow up and be taken care of by men who were ambitious.

But I have a need to work. I'm very itchy if I'm not working. There are certain jobs I won't do. I refuse to be a dental hygienist. I'd like to do more comedy movies. Humor was a priority in our household. My father was brilliant at it. Humor makes me feel I can get out from under myself. It's a way to get away from people's expectations of me. When I'm funny, I feel free.

It's boring to be with people who have preconceived notions about me. There are people who think I'm aloof, cool, the ice queen. I don't want to be considered on a cosmetic level. I know when people circle me for inspection. It's very constricting. Some seem very relieved that I'm not perfect. But I don't worry about that anymore. I worry about it less when I'm being funny. So do the people watching me. They're not so frozen by mundane expectations.

Shirley MacLaine

on spontaneity

If you're a cynic, forget Shirley MacLaine's strange mystic prattle about achieving the "higher self," lighting the "divine spark," and becoming one of the "children of light."

Her crypticness, though marvelously colorful, is merely her second language. Her first and best tongue is plain English. Especially when it comes to trumpeting the importance of being spontaneous. No one speaks of spontaneity more sincerely, more simply or with more sureness than Shirley MacLaine.

Few women are as unabashedly sure of themselves as MacLaine. I use the word *sure* advisedly. MacLaine is not a woman of obvious and imposing ego. She is a sharer, one of those assured women who articulates personal discovery with a clarity, and excitement, that is infectious. Her fancy talk is less mysterious than you might imagine.

The sureness that she espouses—and projects—is having the confidence to give your natural impulses, your instinct, a chance to operate in your behalf. MacLaine's theory is that when you marry sureness and spontaneity, allow them to co-exist in tandem, you have at your disposal the ammunition to operate with the courage of your convictions.

MacLaine is, in fact, living proof that spontaneity works.

Despite the savage rigors and demands of her superstar status, she relies on and trusts the tenor of her actions and reactions. She does not second-guess herself. If things go awry, she doesn't lay all the blame on herself and slip into an indigo mood. She extracts the good from the bad and leaps forward—but not before acknowledging that an error is like a signpost. It tells you what not to do next time around.

I tell MacLaine this is not easy. What's her secret?

Eyes twinkling, she reveals that hidden below the layers of her sureness and her spontaneity is the discipline not to muffle the mechanism of her inner voice, the invisible muse of herself, in favor of logic alone. She listens deeply to the impulsive murmurs of her heart, balancing them with the cool reasoning of her mind.

According to MacLaine's doctrine on spontaneity, sureness is linked directly to rightness. A woman has to believe not only that she has rights but, also, in the rightness of herself.

Fools that we are, we trudge through life trusting only in our brainpower when spontaneity, the tantalizing key to seemingly inaccessible places of personal growth, is within reach. Children show us constantly that we are born spontaneous creatures. When stifling life experiences jade us, we let spontaneity slip from our grasp.

But spontaneity is everlastingly ours. Grab it.

    I'm beginning to be more spontaneous about myself. I act as soon as ideas spring into feeling. I trust my own spontaneity.

The risk is the thrill. It's the expression of the moment without censorship. Spontaneity is not even something you think about. It's the combination of instant idea and instant action. You don't consider the consequences.

I used to be afraid of "consequences." I'm a middle-class Southern Baptist. The name of the game was either "look before you leap," or, "when in doubt, don't." Sometimes you have to turn your education and conditioning on its ear on purpose. I did. At first I told myself to be cautious. Then I realized that caution is the enemy of spontaneity.

There is a reality to the unseen. Feelings are invisible. Energy is invisible. Intuition is invisible. God is invisible. And spontaneity is invisible. The impact of these invisibles becomes visible, and that's reality.

Of course I believe in magic. But I also believe we create our own magic. We create our own illusions. Magic is illusion, isn't it? When you create negatives, it's called black magic. Most people want light magic or white magic. When you master illusion, that is magic too.

People who have problems with me have problems with their own sense of reality. I'm not controversial to me. I know what I think. I'm not conflicted. And I'm not messianic about my beliefs. I'm not a fundamentalist. I don't think I have a hot line to heaven.

I struggle to be understood. Doesn't everyone?

Everyone mirrors everyone. The things we find despicable about other people are reflections of things we find despicable about ourselves. When I do something about the despicableness in me, the other person becomes less despicable.

I also believe in the masculine intelligence of the brain and the feminine intelligence of the heart. The feminine intelligence is the energy of nurturing, of allowance, and of tolerance.

These are unseen powers. They are invisible. The masculine energy is assertive energy. It is militant. It consists of anger, the barricade psychology and the attitude, "I'm not going to take it anymore." Feminine intelligence is based on harmony. Nature is harmonious. It evolves.

I don't have one guide. I have many guides. But my main guide is me. I go by my instinct, my heart, my experiences. When I make mistakes, I say: "Oh, crap, why did I do that?" I analyze my actions and reactions and I ask myself why did I draw that situation to me? I always get an answer from myself.

I really think people can make things better for themselves. Everyone has the power to get off the victimization wheel. You have to ask yourself: "Why am I putting up with it? Why am I still here?"

People can change their lives by accessing their own energies. It's not enough to have a dream. You have to ask yourself hard questions. "How much do I believe in myself? How much tenacity do I have? How disciplined am I?"

Too often people define themselves by their own limitations. I think that sometimes people should step out of their own way. They should take a leap in spontaneity.

Marlee Matlin

on being deaf

Marlee Matlin's interpreter is in absentia and she's mad. Her eyes flash the rage she feels. She indicates she wants the photo session over quickly. She makes me understand that she's on a tight schedule, that she needs to change clothes. Actually she wishes I wasn't there.

But she reads lips well and I tell her, slowly and sincerely, that I understand and not to worry, that we'll work out the interview. She calms down. Matlin's senses are highly tuned. She seems to hear silent vibrations that escape most ears, like my heartbeat and the emanations of my spirit, maybe even my brain. She is osmosis itself.

This all happens in a split second.

When her interpreter, Jack Jason, finally arrives at her Boston Harbor Hotel suite, when she understands that he was caught in a traffic jam at Boston's Logan Airport, she bursts into applause and, via sign language, she asks him to order my favorite drink for everyone: tea. I never told her I liked tea. She could just as well have ordered coffee.

Once Matlin is able to use sign language and her interpreter interprets her answers to my questions, the interview flows swiftly. Matlin is bright and beautiful. The one thing she wants to tell women, especially deaf women, is that they must strive to be their own best friends.

What she means is that any woman, hearing impaired or not, must be kind to herself, accepting of herself, take care of herself, believe in herself, love herself, not only dream for herself but achieve her own dreams. She has done all this. The ride was bumpy, full of road-blocks. Matlin takes the attitude that if she did it, so can you—so can any woman.

Matlin, who lost her hearing at eighteen months after a bout with roseola, won an Academy Award for her 1986 role as the deaf woman in *Children of a Lesser God* opposite William Hurt. She was the young-est recipient of an Oscar for Best Actress and the fourth actress to win an Oscar for a first screen performance. Matlin also won the 1986 Golden Globe Award for Best Dramatic Actress.

Born in Morton Grove, Illinois, Matlin is a 1983 graduate of John Hersey High School in Arlington Heights, Illinois. She studied crimi-nal justice at the William Rainey Harper Community College in Pa-latine, Illinois (1983-84). But she played a role in *Children of a Lesser God* at Chicago's Immediate Theater Company (1985) and, after an international search, won the lead role in the movie version.

Matlin, who'd been acting for years in children's theater for the deaf in Chicago and the Midwest, left the world of law forever.

It was not an easy leap. But she became what she wanted to be-come: an actress.

Matlin had to work on, polish, her attitude. She's the first to tell you that she had a terrible chip on her shoulder, that she felt sorry for herself, that she gave her parents a hard time. She's also the first to tell you that a deaf woman, or any woman for that matter, can accomplish nothing of importance if she doesn't believe she can.

This is what it took Matlin to develop her belief system.

> I was angry at being deaf. I was angry at my parents. They took a lot of crap from me. I had money. I had a car. But I never kept my curfews. I told my parents: "Don't tell me what to do." I thank them for the way they handled me. They let me lead my own life. That was the beginning of my indepen-dence.
>
> I didn't understand me. I had temper tantrums. I swore too much, way too much. I'm always apologizing for swearing. Even

now I have to clean up my mouth. It was just that I thought of myself as a loser.

Kids made fun of my deafness. In our neighborhood, there were two groups. There were the young kids who like to read and tell stories. There were the older kids who played softball on the street and, later, sat around and talked between themselves. There were members of each group who hated each other.

I liked being with the younger group. One day the leader of the older group made fun of me for being friends with such young kids. I got fed up with her attitude. I was in a bad mood. So I went over to her and said: "I have many friends in both groups. Maybe you don't."

It was a good thing, this confrontation. I had faced the reality of a conflict. Everything was out in the open. Let me tell you what motivated me: I didn't want to be known as the only deaf person in the neighborhood. I wanted to be belong. I wanted friends.

To this day, I confront negative situations—but only if there's a good reason. I'm still confronting why I have this desire to face up to things. Maybe tomorrow I'll know better about the art of confrontation. I don't understand it thoroughly now.

In high school, I fell in with a bad crowd. Some good people tried to pull me back with them. I said: "No! No!" It was my rebellious period. I rebelled against everything. I said ridiculous things. I did ridiculous things.

After high school, I went back to the stage. The audience watched me. I watched me. I felt a link between me and them. That's when I began to appreciate myself.

I felt a bonding with the audience. It wasn't a perfect bonding. Nothing is perfect. But I felt good about it. I felt good about myself. Now, everyday, I'm learning how to feel more good about myself. That's how I'm learning to be my own best friend.

I realized I had been given a lot of opportunities.

I'd gone to summer camp. I had gone to the theater after school. I had taken trips. I thought: "Maybe I should appreciate all the good things I've had!" That thought hit me like lightning when I stood there on the stage, looking out at an audience looking up at me. That was really a turning point in my life.

I'm in the communications business. A person who is deaf has a total lack of communication. I grew up using body language and facial expressions. I was very judgmental. I could sense if someone was mad, glad or sad. But I couldn't define, articulate, how they felt.

Once I said to my mother: "Why doesn't everyone sign? Everyone speaks. To sign is to know another language." She said she couldn't answer that, but my question made her feel helpless.

When I was growing up, I hated rules. I still do. I was independent. But my parents paid a lot of attention to me because, I was hearing impaired and, second, because I'm pretty. Being hearing impaired is difficult to accept. I had a lot of hearing friends. Hearing kids could talk on the phone, listen to music, listen to everything. Deaf kids live in a world of silence. Some of my deaf friends were treated preferentially. I certainly was.

I had nice clothes. I had toys. I always carried the neatest lunch bag. But the most important thing I had was my dream. I held on to that dream. My dream was to be an actress. I still have dreams.

Once I told someone my dream of being an actress, and that person said: "It won't happen." I was shattered. I felt as if that person had stabbed me in the heart. I said to myself: "Okay, I won't prove my dream to you. I'll prove my dream to myself."

This is where I found myself tested. You've heard me say I love individuals who are their own best friends. I am my own best friend. I had to be—or how else could I hold on to the dream? It took me a long time to understand myself. I went through a lot. But a lot of good things have happened to me.

There is an emotional pain to deafness. For me, it was feeling like an alien. That's changed. Perhaps my success as an actress has changed. Even today when I see a deaf child, I want to say: "There's nothing wrong with you." I, like that deaf child, happen to be a human being with a handicap. But every human being has a handicap of some sort. To the deaf child, I say three things: Don't feel out of place. Stay with your dream, no matter what. And always be yourself.

Independence is very important. Independence means having freedom and taking responsibility for that freedom. I trusted what I was doing. I believed in myself. That felt good. Freedom is a state of mind, a state of being, and a state of spirit. When all three aspects fall together, the freedom becomes a self-power.

The most important aspect of independence is becoming your own best friend. I don't take life for granted. I don't take myself for granted.

Dyan Cannon

on loving yourself

Dyan Cannon, a blond sprite with a halo of helter-skelter curls, makes a graphic gesture. She raises her right arm and kisses herself just below the elbow.

Cannon, who married the late Hollywood idol Cary Grant when she was twenty-seven and he was sixty-one, generally does not go around kissing herself. Any man would gladly queue up to kiss Cannon, an ageless beauty who oozes come-hither charm. But that's not the point of her kiss.

Cannon is a self-made expert on what she calls "self-realization," a state of mind that is not attainable if you don't love yourself. Hence the symbolic kiss. Cannon's kiss, as light as a feather, comes from a heavy background of many types of therapy. One of Cannon's houses even had a padded cell designed for primal screams. All the yelling didn't work. Nothing worked. That is, nothing worked until she learned to love herself in a healthy, positive way. It took a lot of hurting for Cannon to understand that the Biblical commandment—love thy neighbor as thyself—implies that loving yourself first is a heavenly given.

What led Cannon to the demonstrative kiss were two crises that shook her to the core and, in essence, temporarily destroyed her life.

One involved Cary Grant, their tumultuous three-year marriage and a bitter divorce. There were rumors that Grant had fits of uncontrollable temper and that he beat Cannon who allegedly attributed his behavior to LSD.

On the heels of her divorce, which was bad enough, a professional crisis occurred. Her career plummeted. She began to doubt herself, her abilities, her decisions. Cannon, frozen by frustration and fear, quit acting for three years. She could do that because she's rich. But her money bought her only the comfort of material things. What she wanted most, emotional harmony, was not for sale. It was free. All she had to do was go inward, confront the rumble-tumble of herself.

Cannon's quest was to unblock herself, to unscramble the good memories from the bad, to separate deceptions from truths. Cannon says that during this period she felt like a rat chasing its tail.

We are sitting together in an elegantly appointed suite on the twenty-first floor of an East Side hotel in Manhattan. The room we're in has one glass wall with a view of the city's magnificent skyline. It is noon. Cannon, curled up on the plump cushion of an easy chair, is chomping on carrot sticks and sipping unsweetened herb tea that is served to her on a silver platter by a maid. She is, in fact, the prototypical woman who has everything. But she is a contradiction in terms.

Even when she was at her lowest ebb, when she felt she had nothing of importance, she had much more than most people. But having "everything" is not the same as feeling you have everything—which is what self-realization is all about.

    Life is full of tests and passing tests is passing temptations. Most of us want to be accepted, loved. But these little temptations come up to sidetrack us. If you maximize yourself, you allow the fetters to be removed. You take the limitations away. What limits us is self-doubt. Doubt comes with fear. We're afraid we won't be accepted as part of a group. It's true. Maybe we won't. But we have a choice. We can have the courage of our convictions. Courage is being true to your highest sense of right.

We are faced with choices all the time. We have a little voice in us to direct us, tell us which way to go. But sometimes the little voice does not suggest the popular route. So most of us disregard the little voice, ignoring what it is telling us. Haven't you heard someone say: "If only I'd listened to myself."

A crisis is anything that threatens our joy. We deserve to be happy. I used to think all the action started in front of the camera when the director said: "Action." But how about being "on" all the time? How about enjoying everything? I'm very practical. By that I mean I practice doing things I enjoy. We should not be ripped off from innate joy. When things hurt us, we should throw them out, like the garbage. Metaphysics means above the physical. When I am hurt, I turn to a higher power. Some call it love. Some call it God. But I get in touch with a higher power by going inside myself to a quiet place. When you focus on a quiet place and sit quietly, you listen to your own feelings. It is called staying at one with yourself, listening to your inner voice. It is a strengthener, a stabilizer, a balancing act.

I have had one major career crisis. When I was in Hollywood, I was going from film to film and I was called "successful." I accepted that definition of success. It was success in terms of dollars and I enjoyed it. I didn't listen to an inner voice. I accepted a part that turned out terribly (*Child Under a Leaf*). When I saw it, I was terribly devastated. I had read the script. I had an idea of how it should turn out. But when it was transferred to the screen, it had no substance. That's when I faced the crisis. I said: "This is it! I have more to say than that! There's more to me than that!"

But I didn't understand how to say "no," how to listen to that inner voice. All this did not come to me in one fell swoop. I asked myself how to say "no." And I said: "Just say no, it's not up to my standards." I decided to say that in both a relationship with a man and about scripts. I decided to hold out for what I wanted.

These feelings sort of unfolded over several months. I was faced with temptation. I was associated with success, wealth, fame. And a big French movie director came to Malibu, where I live, offering me a part if I would accept it without seeing the script. I was broke. This was a temptation. But I remembered my promise to myself: "Don't compromise."

My friends said, "Hey, he's a big director. Do you know what you're doing?" But I turned it down, and the people who did it were not happy with the results. That was scarier than anything, that saying "no." But I learned from it. I learned how to trust myself. The more you learn about yourself, the more you can knock fear out of the box of yourself. I was fearful. I said: "No one will love you for saying no. You'll be broke." But I still said no.

I'm whacked all the time. I'm whacked by all the temptations you are confronted with. Sometimes I make it. Sometimes I don't. But now, when I don't, I forgive myself. I muck up, I make mistakes and I tell myself I know better—but I forgive myself. Errors are not forever. We all have to lighten up. I believe we have to treat ourselves gently. We show love to others. Why don't we show love to ourselves?

I believe in love. I'm not talking about physicality. I'm talking about the power of love. I believe love reigns over evil. You go through evil situations, but you must think of life as a rose. As the rose unfolds, it opens up and lets in the light until it reaches maturity, until it has let in the most light. The petals may fall off. But the beauty of the rose remains.

Lady Antonia Fraser

on being a natural feminist

What seems to be a blaring inconsistency about Lady Antonia Fraser, is not.

Look down. Her custom-made English riding boots, geared for toughies, are made for stomping. She's not a wobbler given to tottering. The boots mark her as a woman of combat or, in her words, someone who sees herself as "a strong vessel."

Look up. Lady Fraser has accented her purple Jean Muir caftan, wildly reminiscent of the tender boudoir influence of London's couture, with the sort of exquisitely jeweled tree-of-life pin that you might glimpse in a Tiffany window at Christmas. When she runs her pink manicured fingers through her coiffed hair, her weighty knuckle-size diamond ring blinds you with its radiance.

Lady Fraser is, in fact, exactly what she appears to be: a woman who blends her so-called "masculine" inclination, particularly self-determination, with her glorious femininity.

It was she who created a huge international scandal when she left her husband of twenty years, the late Hon. Hugh Fraser, an aristocratic politician with whom she had six children, for the playwright Harold Pinter.

It's no surprise that she was the subject of media outrage. A story about a married man and "the other woman" isn't nearly as boggling as the explosive story of "the other man" usurping the life of a long-married woman.

All she'd say about her romantic bent to Pinter, and her divorce and subsequent marriage to him, is: "I made a decision, a powerful decision, and I followed through. I have no regrets."

She says what she means and means what she says.

Her chic boots are emblematic of the masculine twist of her personality: the ability to make a daring self-determination, follow her heart and, despite the tiresome consequences, not to relinquish her belief that she, and she alone, is the master of her fate. Her flowing bedroom-inspired dress, and her remarkable jewels, signify the enormous power of her femininity. She didn't sacrifice one for the other.

Even Gloria Steinem has observed that the masculine, bereft of the feminine, is nothing. Lady Fraser is, in her own words, "a natural feminist"—that is, a feminist who is more influenced by her inclinations than by strict feminist doctrine.

It is Lady Fraser's contention, and she certainly put her money where her mouth is, that there are certain human qualities that defy gender.

    St. Paul is on my personal hit list. It was he who decreed that the husband must look after the wife because she is the "weaker vessel." Women are, by nature, spirited and exciting, especially in difficult situations. That is commonplace. My theory is that women are stronger than men. It's simply that they have not been afforded the same opportunities. But when they see opportunity, they seize it with both hands.

In Britain, in the 17th century, the property of the wife went to the husband, and his property remained his property. Though it's not the law today, the notion remains. Women have always been oppressed. In the 17th century, women were nearly 100 percent illiterate. Education is a key to liberation.

My mother was keen on my education. She was a natural feminist, and she made me believe I was equal to my brothers. That was a good start. Many of my contemporaries have achieved a great deal. But, even now, they have never recovered the wonderful feeling that they are equal to men. They grew up accepting an inferiority.

I really don't want to talk about my romantic decisions. But I made a decision, a powerful decision, and I followed through. I don't have regrets. But that is a side of my life I will not talk about. My marriage to Harold Pinter is happy. My husband encourages me. But his privacy is total to him. I respect that privacy. I will tell you that my husband always reads my manuscripts, and I always read his. But that's all I will say on the subject of my marriage.

I've never liked to tackle easy things. That's artistically wrong. And it's not interesting. There has to be a high level of interest there for me. It's the only way to self-maximize. I must always stretch to get to the best part of myself. Otherwise I don't have the petrol, the energy, to do the job.

My work attitude goes back to my mother. She filled me with a feeling of my own worth. I was the oldest of eight children. My mother never confronted me with: "Are you tops in your class? If not, why not?" She always encouraged my independence. I've always wanted to be the one who chose what I wanted to do. My friends laugh at me. I consult them. And then I do exactly as I please.

I'm a keen mother. My youngest child is seventeen. I'm coming to the end of one cycle of motherhood, seeing my children through their education. My next phase is to be a grandmother. That hasn't happened yet.

My daughter once described me as being didactic. She was asked if she meant that I was bossy. But she said she really meant didactic. I was always teaching my children things. I insisted, for example, that they all keep diaries. My children complained that I thus ruined their holidays. But I made them write down their life experiences daily because this was how they would learn to write. Of course I gave them large amounts of cash prizes to do so. Bribes. When my daughter went on her honeymoon to Venice, she startled her new husband by saying: "I have to write in my diary."

What I know of feminism in America is that it was a necessity. The movement had to be pioneered, and Americans organized it. In the beginning, it all seemed radical. But it was a great push forward. There is no such thing as a tame revolution.

American feminism has had impact in England. Now the younger female generation has an overall awareness of its own possibilities. That's quite real. The young men, these women's contemporaries, may not like it. Maybe they would like to encounter women who think they are inferior to them. There are still women who feel that way. Well, let's hope they match up, that they find each other.

In my family, my sons wash dishes along with my daughter. I hope, in marriage, that my sons will not attempt to prove they are all-powerful husbands. I hope they will continue to wash the dishes. I am profoundly feminist. A friend tells me that I talk as if I think women are the first sex. It's just that I don't think women are the second sex.

My contribution to feminism is writing my book [The Weaker Vessel]. I'm an historian. The 17th century is unknown in women's terms. I studied the 17th century for fifteen years. I was able to dig into the undergrowth of women's lives and give philosophers of the current feminist movement a sense of where the 17th century fit into women's history. But I never just sat back and said: "How can I help the feminist movement?" I thought: "How can I rescue unknown women? Over the centuries, women's lives have been ignored.

The ideal 17th-century beauty was blonde. The idea was that fair outside meant fair inside, sweet. Dark women were thought to be impetuous and passionate. The ideal woman of that time was modest and docile. But, of course, women were then what they've always been: stubborn, feisty and strong.

Lately the British newspapers have been full of stories about Brigitte Bardot and Sophia Loren. Loren is thought to be wonderful because she survived a dreadful childhood, carved a career for herself and is a dedicated mother. The current ideal of woman is based on the Sophia Loren image: a strong woman who remains feminine. Apparently, Bardot had a nervous breakdown. She seems to be nobody's heroine because she traded only on her beauty.

I'm very interested in Geraldine Ferraro. Some of the things written about her could have been said in the 17th century. She is expected to be the first perfect politician. Male politicians have never been expected to be perfect. Times have changed. But not enough.

Women fight differently than men. Women have feminine cunning, which is an asset. Women are the underprivileged ones, have observed the master race—men. Women see they can survive by being honorary males and being goddesses at the same time. That's cunning.

Many women have taken a deep breath and pursued careers that have been traditionally male. Anyone who pioneers a new trail is scared inside. But the overriding emotion is inspiration—which is what has gotten women through their initial fears.

The notion of the female ruler is generally distasteful. It's particularly odd that there is no warrior queen, no leader, in the United States—especially since the United States is the home of women's liberties.

In Britain, we are helped by our folk memories of queens as rulers. In American history the heroes aren't heroines.

It was shocking when Mrs. Dole resigned from a significant post to help her husband in his presidential ambitions. Obviously there was a need for partnership. But it was the husband who required the support of a wife. In that atmosphere, a woman cannot be a warrior queen.

When women fought to vote, they were sent to prisons. They went on hunger strikes. They were force-fed. It was ghastly. Some territory was gained. Women were in revolt. But when women win victories, the struggles are too quickly forgotten.

Women always seem to be fighting wars without bloodshed. The biggest war is in the workplace. Perhaps it's because women are still perceived as threatening. Maybe it's enshrined psychology.

But a woman does not have to be dominating to be a warrior. Leadership is one thing. Domination has the nasty quality of force. You can't answer back a dominator. I wish women would remember that.

The original feminists did great work. They made themselves heard. Feminists continue to be militant. It's because they look back on the sufferings of women. Women are prisoners of their history. All causes need militants to support them. But the strident militancy has calmed down.

Modesty is not a good quality when leading troops. People don't follow people who are outwardly apologetic.

People have said I'm a born writer. Nonsense! I'm a born worker. Talent is genetic but it requires industry.

Some people enjoy idleness. I enjoy hard work. It brings me happiness. I have a sense of mission about my work. The pursuit of a project is the joyful part.

If my work is well-received, it's a double bounty. It if isn't, I concentrate on the joy of having done it rather than the result.

There is such a thing as a success attitude. For a moment you have to believe, with all your heart, that you can do what no one else can do. You have to feel unique. But only for a moment. You can't feel like this all the time or you appear unpleasant, even arrogant.

Now women want fulfillment in every area. Women have become more ambitious. But they think there's more to life than careers.

Women have become more appreciative of past generations of women. There's more interest in the matriarchal impulse. There's a new appreciation of the grandmother or the mother who made cookies, hooked rugs and sent us to school looking beautiful.

These women were intelligent and clever. We have a new respect for them because they're also repositories of female history. It is from them that our own perceptions have evolved.

My first husband was a parachutist in the war. He jumped into occupied Belgium. Once I said to him: "You are brave to jump." He replied: "I'd be brave if I said to the sergeant who had us lined up that I won't jump."

You can be shamed into being brave. Even shame can become inspiring. Women shamed into feeling like underdogs have said they won't jump when they're told to jump.

That is continuing.

Françoise Gilot

on obedience

Françoise Gilot is blunt.

Her tone is edged in ice. Her stare is a glare. Her nose is tilted to the ceiling. She is putty in the hands of no one. That was the trouble that created the huge chasm of discord that forever separated Françoise Gilot from Pablo Picasso. She didn't give an inch to Picasso because she knew he'd take a mile.

The tumultuous nine years they lived together, from 1944 to 1953, were marked by howls of dissonance. If Picasso was the king of modern art, Gilot, also a talented painter, believed that she was the queen. It wasn't only that they became competitive. Their personalities clashed because their sexual politics clashed.

Gilot wanted to exist without restrictions. Picasso fenced her in. Gilot became resentful. Picasso, even more agitated by the disharmony between them, strove to possess her. Gilot protested. Picasso burned her right cheek with a cigarette to brand her as his property. Gilot walked out. Picasso, given to fits of jealousy, confiscated all her belongings—even her letters from their mutual friend, Matisse.

Together Picasso and Gilot produced a daughter, Paloma, the famous fashion designer, and a son, Claude, a photographer. But keeping the family together was not a sufficient reason for them to remain under the same roof. Even now, Gilot is nervous when she speaks of Picasso. But in voicing the details of their dissimilarities, she is clear about one fact: she survived Picasso.

Eventually, Gilot married and divorced another artist, Luc Simon, and, still later, she married Dr. Jonas Salk of polio vaccine fame and became his widow. But it is Picasso she talks about. It is Picasso who used the force of his chauvinism against her. It was Picasso who tried to shape her will by the strength of his will rather than by her innate willingness. It is Picasso, the father of her two children, whom she cannot erase from her sphere of awareness.

There's a very good reason beyond their time together.

Picasso was forty years her senior when they met and fell in love. What tripped up their relationship is that Gilot, a woman in love, went to Picasso to be free of her father's control. She thought that Picasso, who was old enough to be her father, would be to her everything her father was not. Gilot was wrong. She jumped from the frying pan into the fire. Picasso was as much the controlling chauvinist as her patriarch.

Picasso demanded obedience. Her father had demanded obedience. Obedience, in fact, became the issue.

That's when her motto became "To thine own self be true."

      I'm a feminist who doesn't hate men. I'm for women's rights, but if you're interested in women's rights, you have to accept the responsibilities.

Yes, I was in competition with my father. He wanted me to go to law school. He wanted me to understand discipline. He said: "Do eight hours of law study and eight hours of painting. That will leave you two hours for physical exercise and five hours for sleep."

He said: "Do what I want you to do, and you can also do what you want to do, paint." I did as he wished until I was twenty-one. But, at age twenty-one, I said: "I no longer have to be obedient." I said: "I've had enough." By that time, I was sure I was a gifted artist. I refused to delay my career. So I went to live with my grandmother.

The challenge between my father and me prepared me for

the challenge between Picasso and me. Both my father and Picasso expected brilliance and obedience from me. I left Picasso when I was thirty-one. I said: "I've proven myself enough. Now it is time for me."

When you made a move against Picasso, you took a risk. He was domineering. I knew that if I crossed him, I would suffer. But our life together was no longer positive. So I left.

Picasso was vindictive. Anything that belonged to me in the house we shared disappeared. What does it matter? If I had thought about it too much, Picasso would have accomplished the result he wanted: my madness. He wanted to destroy me. If I didn't agree with him, I became Public Enemy Number One.

Suffering never stopped me. I have discovered that suffering is not all bad. Suffering enhances your art. When you suffer, you have greater understanding of life. Suffering reveals what is essential in life. Picasso thought this was true.

Matisse did send me letters addressed to Saint Françoise. But only on the name day of Saint François. Matisse didn't think of me as a saint for putting up with Picasso's moods. It was his way of wishing me a happy Saint's Day. On the other hand, they were rivals. Matisse was not immune to challenging Picasso. They played the game of one-upsmanship.

We had what you might call a professional triangle. Matisse and Picasso were friends, and I joined them and we became a trio. The food of the artist is discussion. We had many discussions and many differences of opinions. Some artists try to uncover new aspects of the truth. That was Matisse. Some artists invent new languages. That was Picasso. Both Picasso and Matisse were obsessed with their work. An artist obeys an inner necessity: passion.

They discovered in me someone of both a different generation and someone with opposing opinions. I was not about to change my opinions to please them.

Picasso wasn't really jealous. He was being witty when he said to me: "For you, Matisse is a saint who can do no wrong, and you spend time burning incense at his feet." I replied: "So do you."

Both Picasso and Matisse were obsessed with their work. This was especially true of Picasso. Yet Picasso's jealousy of Matisse was always simmering. Yes, Matisse wanted to paint me. Matisse knew that Picasso would be displeased by the suggestion. It was a bit of a provocation on Matisse's part. Picasso reacted by being upset.

But it was an intellectual game. I was the prize. The very first time Picasso introduced me to Matisse, Matisse suggested painting my portrait. It was Matisse's way of saying I had beauty. Picasso didn't like that. Picasso started making portraits of me himself. When Matisse did a portrait, you sat for him. When Picasso did a portrait, it was done from his imagination.

You can be the spectator of yourself. I can look at myself from without as well as within. I am quite objective about myself. I am unusual. I have more talent and more imagination than most people. I am as interesting in my way as the men in my life are interesting. As an artist I don't hope to please people. I hope my work gives them insight. An artist sees the world through the eyes of love or hatred. It's the same thing. Hatred, in art, means the artist sees something that needs to be changed. It is constructive criticism, which is like love in wanting to make things better.

Picasso was not the best part of my life. He was interesting intellectually. He was not fulfilling emotionally. Now I don't have Picasso paintings in my life.

What had been positive between us was our work. We disagreed on human terms. He was a womanizer. That was not the only aspect that made our life together disagreeable. I cannot tell you more. Let's leave it at that.

Wendy Wasserstein

on being a girl

When Wendy Wasserstein, a wildly successful woman with her name up on the marquee, told me she loved being a "girl," I flipped. She was entering her forties. But I forgave her instantly. I thought: "Oh dear, it's just a slip of the tongue."

After all, Wasserstein had won a Pulitzer and a Tony for writing the smash Broadway hit, *The Heidi Chronicles,* a dazzling study of feminism. She has, in fact, addressed the frayed side of feminism by articulating a litany of paradoxical issues in the form of rhetorical questions.

Why don't women recognize the continuing poison of inequality as the reason they occasionally sabotage each other in the mad scramble for too few important jobs? Should she choose a man to father a baby without committing to either a relationship or a marriage? And what would her mother think of that? And the issue at hand: Why should she be known as a woman when she sometimes feels like a girl?

As far as I know, the word "girl" is not in the current feminist language except for preteens. Even that may be stretching the point, given the current sociological phenomenon of babies having babies.

I didn't call her on the girl issue until Wasserstein, who's built like a lovable-huggable teddy bear, used the word *girl* six times in six minutes.

Well, well. It turns out that the legendary feminist with ruggedly independent thoughts on feminism thinks it's a very good idea for women to think of themselves as girls. Tell me why, I said. Before

Wasserstein started sharing very explicit girl stories on herself, she prefaced her contention that women should be more like girls because girls are less shrewish than women. This is the gist of her theory:

Girls are endlessly energetic. Girls aren't pretentious. Their outlook isn't jaded. There's a freshness about them, a naïveté that hasn't canceled out, or dwarfed, the wellspring of hope. Girls can appear naive and yet be the source of a deliberate surprise action that sets off chaos that can lead to change. Girls don't have conditioned responses, they create their own responses.

Wasserstein, who lives with her cat, even told me that she writes wearing a Lanz flannel nightgown and, if it's cold, tosses a Dartmouth sweatshirt over it. Girls are, by nature, unconstricted creatures. Besides, when she suffers anxiety attacks she eats pizza, eats chocolate, eats cookies. Girls exercise their eating freedoms.

Okay, we were two girls having a friendly argument. That didn't stop me from telling Wasserstein that her idea of girlishness, with its combination of sublime innocence, sunshine outlook and sense of fun, was more romantic than real and that I didn't believe a word of what she was saying.

Oh, yeah? Wasserstein said and proceeded to detail some girlish mischief she stirred, the brilliant prank she played on her high school headmistress who said that "girls" go to college to find a man, not a career. Wasserstein, a graduate of Mount Holyoke College and the Yale School of Drama, described the incident, and her girlish method of retaliation, which she reveals in this interview, as "freeing."

To be a girl is to be audacious enough to indulge in girlish pranks to make a point.

Okay, I said, what's the difference between how a girl reacts to limitations and how a woman reacts? I also pointed out that she was a young woman, not a "girl," when she was in high school. Oh, pooh, she said giggling. Women are natural antagonists, saboteurs. They're jealous of other women and their successes and they can be cut-throat and mean. They're naughty little girls, she said.

Prove it, I said.

And Wasserstein did.

Once, at a meeting of Jewish feminists, a woman stood up and said: "Do you think the ending of your play is correct?" My play ends with Heidi adopting a Latin American infant.

Well, well, I thought: "Is there a correct ending to anything?" It was as if the woman had said to me: "If you don't see it from my point of view, you are wrong." I got extremely defensive. Another woman even asked if I wrote the ending of my play to be commercial! When I'm angry, my voice drops four octaves. It dropped five octaves. I told the woman I wrote that play in a cold rooming house in London with a $4,000 grant.

Obviously it was not a basic get-rich scheme done in an elegant set of rooms by the sea. I've given my life to writing plays about women, and women sit there and turn on me and my plays.

After I won the Pulitzer, a woman friend stopped seeing me. Maybe it was jealousy. Maybe I turned out to be someone she thought I wasn't. The friend's perception of me was altered. Just before the friend dropped me, she said: "Your life is all about career. I'm interested in motherhood."

I don't look back at feminism with anger. I'm a feminist, but I'm also interested in other things. Oh God! You want to know what I really think? I think the fight for equality isn't over. There are limited slots open. That's why women fight with each other! For those slots.

In high school, the American dream girl was the cheerleader. In the world of careers, the American dream girl is a skinny girl in a short black suit. I never thought of myself as a pretty girl in a party dress. I'm just a funny person who's actually very serious. I use humor to be accepted. If I was Jane Pauley and I had to sit with Deborah Norville, I'd go crazy. I'd get weepy and leave. Or my wit would become sharper and sharper until it got pointed. I would not want to be in a competitive situation with other girls.

I had a headmistress in high school who told me that girls went to college to get a Mrs. degree. I was angry at her. I thought: "What is this?" I didn't answer her in words. I answered her in behavior. I did whatever I could to irritate that woman. I went to class wearing large work shirts outside my skirts. I didn't sit in my seat. I slumped.

That woman talked to my mother about my grooming. That woman also told my mother that I was a leader and she was worried about which way I'd lead people! I suppose it was because I once instigated my entire class to cut school for one day. My reaction to that woman wasn't verbal. It was a continuing show of independence, of strength, of eccentricity. That was how I responded to her. I have a lot of trouble with pretentious people. I always wonder what the pretense is covering.

I can get very down. I don't want to be next year's forgotten person. I get scared about my next play. I get scared of Wendy backlash, of people saying: "Yeah, we know her and we're tired of her." I'm even scared that people will think that Heidi is a drip.

So I get anxiety attacks and I eat as much as possible. I go to John's Pizza. I eat chocolate. I eat cookies. I eat bad things. Afterwards I feel guilty. But it's thrilling while I'm eating.

When I was twenty-seven, I had a boyfriend who said that if my play went to Broadway, he'd leave me. He said: "I just won't be around!" It was a threat. God knows this man was a lawyer who later wrote plays and sent them to my producer. I was shocked!

If I was a man, I'd be an arrogant man now. Sometimes I'm selectively arrogant. I'm arrogant when arrogance is needed. There are times I actually see myself as a woman. I say: "Honey, I've been there! I've seen it! So what's the problem?"

But I write in a Lanz flannel nightgown with a Dartmouth sweatshirt over it. It's my nonconstricting outfit. Besides, there is a continuum to it. That's the way I wrote when I was sixteen. There's something freeing about being a girl.

Sally Field

on being a pragmatist

Gossip columnists had a field day when Sally Field was having an affair with Burt Reynolds.

Field took a practical approach to the sensational trivia, the blare of bad publicity that could have cast serious aspersions on her, personally and professionally. She ignored the press who wouldn't ignore her. By that I mean she didn't read the reports in the first place.

"I never took a look when I thought I wouldn't like what I saw," she says matter-of-factly. This is a generic Field philosophy that touches everything in her life.

Field, who's in her early fifties and still looks like a petite cross between Gidget and The Flying Nun, is the prototype pragmatist. She is down-to-earth and practical, someone who snatches the moment, lives it to its fullest, and turns her back on undue criticisms and unwarranted rumors.

Her protective armor, much more obvious to the observer than she thinks, is based on overcoming a lingering image of "cute."

Field is very specific on this issue.

She has never wanted the world to think of her as "cute." In Hollywood, only superlatives count. You have to be beautiful, flawlessly beautiful, or you are second-rate. Sally Field is cute. But she's much more. She's sophisticated, strong, and comedic. "To me, *cute* was synonymous with being mindless. I don't feel that anymore. Now I think it all depends on who calls me cute," she says merrily.

It has taken a lot of effort and courage for Field to go from cute to acute, to go from giggly ingenue to a serious actress who has won two Oscars and an Emmy.

She had to make a practical move by taking matters into her own hands.

In one fell swoop, she fired her agent and her business manager, divorced her husband, ditched Hollywood and went to New York City to study at The Actor's Studio. The people she cut out of her life had no respect for her abilities, her talents and, most of all, her potential. Field figured if she didn't make a total escape, she would always be stuck with the status quo. She overturned her life in order to turn herself around.

It's one thing to do this, and it's quite another to do this and not to heed the naysayers, the detractors.

What I liked and respected about Sally Field, and her method of making a molehill out of her mountain, is that she didn't acknowledge anything or anybody who presented a point of view that she might not like.

     ✎   I have highs and lows. I've gotten through my lows by kicking and screaming. Sometimes I've gotten depressed. Analysis has helped because it's talking to someone who understands how the human psyche works. I always try to ride things out by figuring things out. And subconsciously I dedicate myself to productive pursuits. I do something. I fix something. The idea behind the idea is to make things better. I apply myself to turning a negative into a positive. Allowing yourself to feel negative is to feel anti-life.

But understand this: I don't see life as lived on a big scale. I've always taken one step at a time. It's one day at a time.

The energy and intensity of me are part of the package of me. But if I seem to be a strong person, it's because I have a terrific mother. She has always liked me, as well as loved me, and she has always told me the truth regardless of my truth.

At the baseline level of me is the great gift my mother gave me: a sense of my own worth. My mother has always been loving, supportive and honest with me.

I'm a pragmatist almost to the point of nausea. I don't have big dreams because I get frozen behind those big dreams. Dreams always look awesome to me. They stupefy me. I like to work things out day by day.

As a person, I'm totally realistic. I live for the days. It's an innate personality trait. It's not that, as a kid, I set my heart on a big Christmas and didn't have a big Christmas and said to myself: I'll never plan a big Christmas again. This is just the way I am.

As an actress, I'm fanciful.

I have an enormous fantasy life. It's a side of my vision that has always been there. The fancifulness of me is ignited properly in me through acting. It is my launching pad. In person, I have the fantasy under control. The flight of fantasy is a gift someone once gave me, something I never asked for, something that is now the foundation of my acting technique.

I've never thought of winning, of achieving, or proving anything. I just go after the big thrill: acting. But acting is all about text. Suppose you haven't eaten for three days. If you eat a bowl of shredded paper, that's no thrill. But if you eat a glorious meal, topped by a hot fudge sundae, cappuccino and brandy, the text has been satisfying. To an actor, the text has to feel like a good meal: very substantial.

The energy and intensity of me are part of the package of me.

The biggest challenge of my life is fulfilling all the requirements I've set up for myself. I don't have priorities. That's because I want everything. I don't want to give up my children for a relationship, or my relationship for my children, or my career for a home, or my home for a career. This is not easy. That doesn't bother me. "Easy" bores me. I get so caught up in the day's work and its demands that the challenge is simply getting things done.

I've had three good roles so far in my career: Sybil, Norma Rae, and Edna [in *Places In The Heart*]. Three times, for me, the character was so whole that acting was a revelation, like an out-of-body experience. Acting is my identity. It's tied up with my vision of myself. The joy of acting is the chance to actually become someone else. It's like somebody else is living inside you.

I've always wanted to be taken seriously, not as a short, cute person, but as a person. There were years that I didn't like to be called cute. To me, cute was synonymous with being mindless. I don't feel that way anymore. Now I think it all depends on who calls me cute.

I think things happen to you when you're ready. Your vision changes. You become receptive to situations. You recognize qualities in people and feelings. In a relationship, sometimes one partner is stronger than the other. But as the situations of life shift, so do the strengths. The partners end up learning from each other's strengths.

Estée Lauder

on extemporaneousness

The first time I met Estée Lauder, she sneered at my pale pink lips, grabbed a raucous red lipstick from a gold stand sitting on her elaborately ornamented Louis-The-Something desk, strutted over to where I was still standing, my winter coat still on and my briefcase in hand, and with no warning, wordlessly smeared my lips scarlet.

Because her hand wasn't steady, or because my back-away reflexes responded instantly, she went far beyond my lip line. I glimpsed the ridiculous zigzag mess when I jerked my head away and caught a look at myself in one of the big rococo mirrors punctuating her ivory moiré walls. The cosmetics giantess, in her natural habitat, thought of herself as the queen of all she surveyed. We were in her elegant on-high office on Fifth Avenue with its stunning view of the skyline that stretched to infinity.

I'm telling you this incident in slow motion. In reality, it happened about a second after our introduction and it was over in a second. But it's stuck forever in the annals of my memory. This wasn't about red lipstick. It was about Estée Lauder's love of extemporaneousness.

Mrs. Lauder, as she liked to be called, retired long ago from the worldwide $2.9 billion empire that she built. Now I can tell you what I thought then: that her initial gesture to me, a young fashion editor, was astoundingly nervy, pushy, arrogant, impudent and overbearing. I was embarrassed. Angry, too.

I remember how coolly she appraised me as I reached into my purse, retrieved a tissue and wiped away any trace of lipstick. Mrs. Lauder didn't apologize. She told me that I looked better in red lipstick, that it perked up my face, balanced the drama of my eyes. I thought of Mrs. Lauder not as a tycoon but as a car salesperson in disguise.

I also thought I'd never like this strange cosmetic-crazed creature who always seemed to be stretching her neck like a crane, which I later learned was an exercise to keep her skin tight. I especially didn't like her custom-designed hats, pillboxes or toques that coordinated perfectly with her suits because they were made from the same fabrics. Everything about her seemed contrived, even her adaptation of her real name: Josephine Esty Mentzer.

I pushed the red lipstick issue out of my mind. Instead, I asked Mrs. Lauder about her wild inclination to free-will actions. We were still wary of one another. Later, in a series of interviews stretched over a number of years, she became a little more open about her life as a woman versus being the Giantess. When her husband Joseph Lauder died, she was particularly frank about their divorce, which she called "a mistaken impulse," and their remarriage.

She was eighty or so when we last met. She strung together a series of small secrets connected to the big one: operating on impulse. Mrs. Lauder didn't say good-bye. When we parted she told me to remember that ad-libbing life was a good thing.

There's no such thing as an old lady. I feel young. I work every day. I never tell my friends I'm too tired to do things. I have energy. I eat. I have a good breakfast, a nice lunch and a light dinner. Too many people in this world are on diets. They lose weight and they lose strength.

One woman friend recently said to me: "Look, I lost two inches on my hips." So who's going to notice things like that? A woman's face is her fortune. There's no holding women back these days. There are only women who don't care. They hold themselves back. Not everyone was born beautiful as

Brooke Shields. But she takes time to look even more beautiful. I always take time for myself.

I wanted to be an actress. Love interfered. Besides, I always wanted to fix up everybody's face. I thought I could make everyone beautiful. People who succeed have a goal. Ultimately, my goal was to make people more beautiful than nature intended.

I had a great love for my husband. Those last years together we were inseparable. I talk to him every day. I'm not crazy. It's just that I imagine he's still with me. It's just that I miss him so much. I miss the great balance he gave my life.

A wife should remember that her husband has endured difficulties in the office during the day. When my husband came home, I was always wearing fresh clothes and fresh makeup. I wore a big smile too. If you can't flirt with your husband, who else is there?

Women who divorce remember all the bad things. They forget they might have been at fault. The divorce [in 1939] was my fault. I wanted to go out, to be with many people. A friend told me: "You're so pretty. You could get anybody."

I wish I'd never listened. But really, in my heart, my husband was always my husband, even when we were apart. I regret my divorce. It would have been better if I hadn't gotten divorced at all. But, I suppose, everything happens for a reason. When we got back together again [in 1943], things got better between us. From then on we stayed together through thick and thin.

To keep a son happy, you have to be good to his wife. Even if you have one pair of good earrings, give them to your daughter-in-law. Tell her: "These are mine, they're precious to me, but I want you to have them." That's how you make yourself a second daughter versus a daughter-in-law.

Women are jealous of other women who are big successes. You can't really deal directly with jealousy. I know, though, jealousy can't be ignored. It's so insidious ... jealous people are ugly people. To them I say: "This success of mine didn't come easy. I didn't get it by dreaming about it." The jealousy doesn't go away, of course. But, at least, it silences it for a moment.

Luck has nothing to do with success. It's so ridiculous when people say they've had good luck or bad luck. When I thought I couldn't go on, I forced myself to keep going. There were times I cried a lot. Certain days didn't work. Certain strategies didn't work. Nothing worked.

I had, after all, entered an industry dominated by giants. They thought of me as a little girl, not someone to be reckoned with, not someone to worry about. I persisted. My success is based on persistence, not luck. I worked myself up to the point where the giants really worried about me.

I make creative decisions instinctively. My son makes the business decisions. I create with my sense. I put a fragrance bottle in the palm of my hand. If it feels good to the touch, I accept it for my collection.

I tell women to cream their faces. The first thing a person sees is your face, not your shoes. Women complain there's no time to cream their faces. When I'm in a hurry I take a bath with cream on my face. Busy women know how to do two things at one time.

Mary Higgins Clark

on never giving up

Mary Higgins Clark writes such great bestselling mysteries that she has been called the Queen of Suspense—which, in turn, may have something to do with her $750,000-and-up advances and $1.5 million for paperback rights.

It wasn't always this way. Her first story was rejected forty times. It sold, finally, for a hundred dollars. When that first letter of acceptance came, she put a vigil light under it. She is deeply religious. She storms the heavens with her prayers. When her pleas are answered, she always thanks God for helping her. But she also helps herself. She never gives up when giving up is easy to do.

Clark graduated from secretarial school and worked as an advertising copy writer and a hostess for Pan Am Airlines. But when she was forty-six, she entered Fordham University and graduated *summa cum laude* with a bachelor's degree in philosophy. She immediately threw herself a prom party. The invitation read, in part: "Lo, after these many years, come to a prom twenty-five years overdue." She also knows how to have the last laugh.

What fascinates Clark is the mystery of life, its circuitousness and its fragility. She may be rich and famous now, but she knows what it is to be poor and unknown. Clark, a widow who raised five children on her own, says that life itself is suspenseful and unpredictable and that her best ideas for plot and character come from the things she sees happening around her—and to her.

Clark, who has watched life being snuffed away, considers the specter of death particularly fascinating. Her first husband died while she was giving him mouth-to-mouth resuscitation and her mother-in-law, witnessing the death of her son, dropped dead on-the-spot from shock. Two dead at one time.

Clark, ever curious, has taken courses on reincarnation. She hoped to be convinced that there is life after life. But her attitude is that we have one chance at life and, despite its fleetness, it's up to us to live it to the fullest. That's why Clark never gives up. There's no time to waste.

She talks a lot about counting your blessings. By that she means sifting bad experiences, like the death of loved ones, and extracting a good point. She calls the points "lessons," saying that the lessons we learn are applicable to other areas of our life. She talks about the power of ESP, a strong form of intuition, and says that women are born with deep sensitivities and should not relinquish that power of perception.

The best way to describe Mary Higgins Clark is "sensible." No one chooses the pattern of their life. What counts is how one reacts to ups and downs, especially the downs. If there's one message she has about making a molehill out of a mountain, it's that no matter what happens you must continue, move on.

She did.

We all hang by a thread. When I was ten, I came skipping home from Mass. A neighbor stopped me to announce casually that my father was dead. Dead? I was just a little girl and the fact of life, which is death, confronted me. It was a lesson in human precariousness. You're here one day and you disappear the next. The shock was that just yesterday I had said good night to my dad. I didn't know it was good-bye. Something can happen at any moment. That's what makes life the ultimate mystery.

Some lives flow in an orderly fashion. Some people die

uneventfully at, say, eighty-one. On the other hand, there are those who get turned around in one shattering instant. They aren't looking for trouble. Trouble finds them. Why? That's the mystery. I wish the world were a better place. But, God knows, evil exists.

I go to a lot of trials. Recently, I went to a trial of a man who killed a young nurse who was driving to the hospital at 7 a.m. One block from the hospital, she stopped for a red light. The man jumped in her car and killed her. I thought: "If only she had locked the door. If only." Why was it the nurse's fate to be at that place at that moment? It was a mystery of utter chance.

Another young nurse went to see a friend whose grand-mother was being put in a nursing home. She went on an act of mercy, to see if the old woman needed any help. Her intentions were good. But, it so happened that a neighbor, a killer, was in the house. Then and there, he dragged the nurse down the cellar and killed her. Another mystery of chance.

Last September 22, I was in my New York apartment with my interior decorator. She was sitting at a table eating a sandwich. Suddenly, with panic in her voice, she said: "I have a headache." There was a pause. Even more panic engulfed her as she said: "I can't feel my arm." That was it. She was gone. Dead. She was fifty-one and never had a sick day in her life. I'm fascinated by those moments when something untoward, something shattering happens to people when they least expect it.

My first husband died as I was giving him mouth-to-mouth resuscitation. He was having a heart attack. His mother had just come to visit. She saw it happen. She said: "Oh, Warren!" and she dropped dead. She just collapsed. I didn't mourn her because she always said she didn't want to live beyond her son. I was glad she didn't see her son in the casket. I had five children, ages five to thirteen. Our house had been a happy house. I thought: "I will not moan. I will not be a creep. It would be an insult to his memory to create undue tension in the home."

I think there's life after death. I don't think we're all dressed in white robes up there, singing all the time. But the spirit is immortal. These values are reflected in my writing. I don't write about ghosts. But I believe in the power of ESP. So many things cannot be explained. ESP is one of the great mysteries of life. Maybe people are born with inherited knowledge, inherited memories. Maybe that's déjà vu.

I'm intuitive. I believe I inherited that ability from my mother. She had ESP. When my brother was eighteen, he sent a picture of himself from boot camp. "He has death in his eyes," she said. Six weeks later, my brother was dead of spinal meningitis.

Once I took a course in reincarnation. I watched ordinary people in the class be regressed, by hypnosis, to former lifetimes. I saw people change voice, change attitude and give detailed accounts of past lives. I kept a detailed notebook of the dialogue. I took the course for dramatic impact. I thought I could use reincarnation as a theme in a book. I reject the concept of reincarnation. I think you have one go-round at life and that's it. Maybe it's possible, under hypnosis, to pluck sounds out of the air, tune into other conversational channels. I think every word ever spoken is still out there. Perhaps this is still another dimension of ESP.

There are many things we cannot choose about our lives. It's how we react to the inevitable that counts. My characters are strong. They storm the heavens with prayers. But when calamity strikes, my characters react well. They keep going. They carry on.

Rosalynn Carter

on prevailing

When Rosalynn Carter speaks of her rise from peanuts to politics, it is with quiet pride. When she speaks of Jimmy Carter losing his reelection campaign in 1980, it is with quiet resolution. Everything about Rosalynn is quiet: her clothes, her hairdo, her tone of voice. What isn't quiet is her choice of words about the ramifications of being faulted for being Jimmy's equal partner and feeling that, at last, she has prevailed.

She and Jimmy, whom Rosalynn married when she was eighteen, share a credo: "Do the best you can and don't brood if you lose." But, in truth, Rosalynn brooded when they had to move back to Plains, Georgia. Technically, she didn't lose. Jimmy did. But their lives are so intertwined that what happens to one is keenly felt by the other.

Before returning home, they went back to Camp David one last time. They played tennis. They swam. They even went fishing. They pretended that the big defeat to Ronald Reagan hadn't happened. Rosalynn particularly dreaded leaving Washington. She slipped into an uncharacteristic emotional slump. For months after they moved back to Plains, she wouldn't watch television. The Reagan White House was in the news. They'd lost their big stage but they hadn't lost each other. She and Jimmy cleaned house. She and Jimmy repainted everything. She and Jimmy planted a garden.

Their togetherness fostered a magical healing balm. At last they could talk about the worrisome things that bothered Rosalynn.

The more they talked, the more they realized that one of their problems involved their image as an interchangeable and interdependent couple. America had talked up equality but America couldn't stand it in the Carter White House. Rosalynn had always wanted to speak publicly about this but, until we talked, she mostly kept herself to herself.

Rosalynn flinched particularly hard when the media described her as a "steel magnolia" and it stuck. The implication was that she looked like a delicate flower on the outside but inside she was unflinching and manipulative. She has always wished that she could make people understand that the romance of her marriage was and is based on mutual respect. Their partnership is real because they've made it real.

I had interviewed Rosalynn Carter several times: on the campaign trail, in the White House, and after their return to Plains. The first time we talked, Rosalynn sailed on hope. The second time she sailed on victory. The third time she sailed on, and past, the public rejection that comes with being ejected from the first office of the land by popular vote. Rosalynn was at her best in our last interview.

Early on, Rosalynn had been forced to accept the idea that she was greater in strength than her situation. She was thirteen when her father, a mechanic, died of leukemia. She worked after-school in a local beauty shop giving shampoos. Her mother, postmaster of the local post office, took in sewing. We talked about the art of prevailing.

    I've never really analyzed myself, but I know that growing up I never showed exactly how I felt because I didn't want to disappoint my mother or father. When I married Jimmy, I did the same with him. I never let my anger or hurt out. It was something I learned not to do. Actually I developed a confidence about not taking setbacks or hurt too hard. I just kept pushing forward, no matter what happened.

It never bothered me that the press called me "steel magnolia." I didn't like it, but I was out there. You can be defeated by criticism, so I really started thinking hard about what the phrase "steel magnolia" implied. Steel means strong. Magnolia suggests something southern and genteel. Sometimes you have to accept criticism and not worry about it. Once, though, I told Jimmy we ought to pay attention to criticism, that maybe we could learn something from it. But so much criticism is heaped on you, you tend to slough it off.

There had been a lot of talk about my being Jimmy's equal partner. Southern women have always been at their husband's side. Husbands go with their wives to the grocery store, the drugstore, the bank. Even when I worked in the peanut warehouse, I never felt I was ahead of my time. I felt I was doing what I was supposed to do. When Jimmy ran for governor, the press started asking me about the issues. I didn't even know what the issues were. So I had to ask Jimmy. And that's how the partnership evolved. Never, for a moment, did I think I was doing anything unusual.

I'm not so immersed in Jimmy's personality as people think. But he has always made me believe I can do whatever I set my mind to do. Jimmy never told me I had to learn the issues. But I had seen a lot of political wives left behind, left out. Jimmy never said: "I'm going to run for office. You have to learn the issues." I would have resented that. We sat down and decided everything together. We planned everything we were going to do together. He made me feel I was part of everything he did.

You can be successful just being at home. I'd never come out and say I'm a successful person. But you've asked me how I feel about myself. I'm going to tell you. I have a lot of confidence. That's because I've learned that to accomplish anything you have to be firm about yourself. You can't have self-doubts. You can't doubt what you're accomplishing because, in the end, you have to depend on your own energy. It helps an awful lot if you have people around you who believe in you.

The romance in my marriage comes from mutual respect. Jimmy is always so proud when I do things. He still believes that I can do anything. That's what really makes me love him. I have the same feelings about him. We're never bored with each other.

I felt bitter after we lost the re-election. But I was not bitter forever. Jimmy has a philosophy: "Do the best you can and don't brood if you lose." I've never known Jimmy to brood for one day. I was angry when we lost. Mad. I don't think the press was fair to us during the campaign. Every time we went out on the campaign trail, the press played up some picky negative story about Jimmy Carter. The press never jumped on Ronald Reagan, never exposed his vulnerabilities.

I've discovered that all the resources I had inside the White House are still available to me outside. I can call anybody, anywhere. Losing the reelection was not the end of my career. I still have access to people in the world. I still have an exciting life. I don't have power. But I still have influence.

The picture the world has of feminists is colored by a few vocal, abrasive women. That's not a true picture. A feminist is someone who does what she wants to do, whatever that is. If she wants to stay home and take care of her house and children, she is still a feminist. She's a woman who has a choice, has made a choice and feels that the choice is all right.

Lana Wood

on sibling rivalry

When I became a top nationally-syndicated fashion editor, I lost a lovely friend.

She didn't die. Our friendship died.

To this day, I take full responsibility for initiating the demise. My intentions were the best. I liked her so much that I trusted her too much and, when I gave her a job as my assistant, she went after my job. I discovered that Ms. X, once a sister figure, was a master saboteur and I, her mentor, was her target. Whenever I think of Ms. X, it is within the context of betrayer. She was jealous of me.

Obviously I made an error in judgment. I over-idealized my relationship with Ms. X. I took a personal friendship and transferred it to the workplace thinking that I was building a support system of my choice. In the process of teaching her everything I knew, nurturing her, we became sibling rivals in the office. I had no idea that, more than anything, she wanted to sit where I sat, become the professional I had become.

Office sisters can and do kill each other. It has to do with insecurity, the gnawing feeling that she has more than you do. It is as if keeping up with the Jones has become keeping up with the Joans.

In the course of interviewing Lana Wood, we started talking about the drawbacks of the sisterhood within the feminist movement. One subject led to another. I told her about my experience with Ms. X who, it turned out, went to live and to work in Europe and majored in breaking up marriages.

We started to talk about the degree of competition among women, particularly blood sisters. Lana pointed out how much more intense and complicated it is for real sisters who grow up measuring their beauty, their talents, their achievements against each other. She told me how profoundly difficult it was for her, an actress, to constantly compare herself to her sister, Natalie Wood, the dazzling movie star known round the world.

To understand the fierceness of their feelings toward and about each other, you've got to understand that Lana and Natalie resemble each other—which Lana denies. Lana even sounds the way Natalie used to sound. She has the same dramatic eyes. Even their silhouette is the same, small and taut. But Lana always felt inferior to Natalie. Who wouldn't?

Lana and Natalie had a serious feud that lasted a year. Lana admits she was jealous of Natalie, that she envied her sister's international success, and the trappings that it wrought. Lana thought Natalie had betrayed her. She was angry and wounded. They made up before Natalie's mysterious drowning at age forty-three in November 1981.

Lana asked me if Ms. X had ever talked to me, or vice-versa? I told Lana that the situation got far beyond the point of damage control and Ms. X ran away to another part of the world. Yes, Lana said, there's a point of no return. She and Natalie almost crossed that line. It was Lana who saved the sisterhood.

    I didn't look like Natalie. My features are angular. Hers were soft. I have freckles. She didn't. She had those big brown eyes. I never thought I was pretty. She was pretty. She was my ideal. That's how I measured my prettiness. I'm still not satisfied with myself. I still think I need improvement. I'm always buying new creams. I'm always buying toners for my hair. I have exercise equipment in my house. The only lousy thing I do is smoke.

But I always felt insecure with Natalie. I couldn't go one-on-one with her. I always said: "I'm lesser and that's the way I'm going to stay." I'm still insecure. Of course I was jealous. Absolutely.

I wasn't jealous when we were younger. I wasn't jealous when we went to parties together. I wasn't jealous when we shared the same circle of friends. I wasn't jealous when we traded clothes and hung around together.

Then this happened: When my daughter was born, my husband [Richard Smedley] and R.J. [Robert Wagner], the man Natalie married twice, had an argument. It was between them. But, after that, I didn't see Natalie much. Things were financially difficult for me. I didn't have a cent. Natalie had a big house, a pool, a nanny for the children, a maid. At that time, I was the cook, the cleaner, the bottle washer. I felt envy. I thought to myself: "If I could have what she has for just one week." I tried to squelch the jealousy with logic. I said: "But Natalie earned this." But my feelings weren't assuaged.

People get mad at each other. It takes a long time to get over being mad. I've even gotten mad at some of my best girlfriends and not talked to them for a year or so. Then I'll just call and say: "I don't care what's happened. I like you. Let's be friends again." But that takes time.

Natalie's death was accidental. I don't believe in the new findings that crop up. Maybe the truth of the matter is I don't choose to know anything about those new findings. I think Natalie went to tie up the dinghy, slipped, hit her head, fell, drowned. I prefer to believe she died quickly. There's a terror to thinking someone you love has to suffer terribly to die.

When Natalie died, I was in terrible need to talk to somebody. Therapy was a necessity. The doctor told me to write down everything, good and bad. I was told to write down even things that were best forgotten.

Relationships, all kinds of relationships, are difficult. I think the ideal is to make a commitment, to be best friends to another person. But it's hard. I'd like to have a wonderful marriage, but the difficulties begin to happen. People are different. You cannot ever fill another person's needs completely. It all has to do with expectations. But if you understand the down side of the relationship, the complications, you just might succeed.

Fortunately, I made up with Natalie before she died. It was tough. I tagged after her. I talked to her. I told her I wanted to make up. Finally, she said: "Certain things are under the carpet, gone." I said: "Great." So we sat in her house, at the bar, talking girl talk. That's how we healed the breach: talking.

If I hadn't made up with her, I would have been more devastated when she died. Big sister relationships are difficult. But I loved her.

The last conversation Natalie and I ever had, we threw our arms around each other. We told each other how much we loved one another. We carried on. That was it. That was the last time I saw her alive. I know it would have been worse for me if I hadn't at least that memory.

Louise Fletcher

on deafness

Cruel lightning careened out of the sky, flashed forward, and struck a four-year-old innocent, Robert Fletcher, rendering him deaf for life and blind in one eye. When the world went quiet and stayed quiet, he questioned God, but he didn't blame God. He became the Rev. Robert Fletcher, an Episcopal minister, and married Estelle.

Estelle Fletcher was pronounced deaf before she was a year old and institutionalized when she was nine. It's unclear how or why this happened, except that Estelle was so frustrated at her inability to communicate that she would hold her breath until she turned blue. Everything changed for the better when she learned sign language.

The Fletchers met at Gallaudet University in Washington, D.C., the only university in the world designed exclusively for deaf students. They fell in love, married, and produced four children. They pinned big dreams on Louise, their oldest child who was pretty and precocious. Louise hated the fact that her parents were "different." To make a molehill out of her mountain, she had to learn that her rage could be converted into a motivating force.

But first Louise had to face the taunts outside her home and the silence within it.

You remember Louise Fletcher. She's the lovely actress who won an Academy Award for her role as the malicious, militant nurse in the Jack Nicholson movie *One Flew Over the Cuckoo's Nest*. What makes her forever memorable was her deceptively simple but profound acceptance speech. It was delivered in sign language: "I want to thank my mother and my father for teaching me to have a dream. You are seeing the dream come true."

It is a journalistic rule to be an uninvolved interviewer. It's impossible. I have never been able to probe into a person's emotional life without a profound sense of sharing, respect and appreciation for the privilege of allowing me, a stranger, to see and to record for public consumption their milestone moments.

Louise Fletcher cried when she told me how her parents' deafness almost stunted her emotional growth—but didn't because she didn't let it. I cried too. We cried together, in public, over lunch at Boston's Ritz-Carlton Hotel.

No one noticed except the solicitous waiter who provided each of us a supply of small cocktail napkins to mop up the tears.

The tears we cried didn't contort the face or precipitate sobs. They simply spilled from some well deep inside. The tears were more victorious and triumphant than feel-sorry, and to extol Louise's telling of the wonderful story of herself, and her parents, we even had dessert.

Our interview was a celebration of Louise and the road she traveled to the top.

    When I was five, I was standing on a street corner with my mother. First Avenue and 20th Street, Birmingham, Alabama. I had been to the dentist. My mother and I were using sign language. I noticed a woman staring. I suppose it was a sight to behold, a child and her parent acting their feelings soundlessly, using facial expressions, rapid hand signals. Suddenly, I became protective, defiant about my mother. "It's not nice to stare!" I told the woman. I was angry. At age five, this was my coping process. The woman apologized, disappeared.

To me, it was like having immigrant parents, those who speak the language of the old country. I was desperate for them to be like everyone else, to talk my language. They didn't. There was the pain of isolation. No child likes to be different.

A child wants to conform, to be like everyone else. It's all part of the peer pressure. But there was no getting around it. My parents were different.

Now, looking back, I see I didn't give my parents enough credit. I thought that because they weren't able to communicate, they weren't capable. When I was a child, I thought of my parents as my children. It was role reversal. I made my own rules. How I'd study. Where I'd study. When I'd study. I had trouble in my school life but I never brought my troubles home. In those days, there was a great stigma to being deaf. Deaf was associated with being dumb, unintelligent. I felt a lot of emotional pain. I never had extended conversations with my mother. She communicated the necessities, that I must get up, that breakfast was ready, that it was time to go to school. But we never sat down and "talked" about the places I'd been, who said what, who wore what. No real mother-daughter stuff. I felt left out.

Loneliness, that was the thing. School was a noisy place. I'd go home at three and all I'd ever hear was the clock ticking. It was that silent. I became so accustomed to silence that I still panic in a noisy environment. I have to calm myself. I still remember going to a friend's house, the hustle bustle, the mother talking to us. Then I'd go home to silence. I was jealous.

My mother was sent to the Asylum for the Deaf. It was called an asylum, not a school, a state-run place, 1909, Austin, Texas. My mother was nine, a little animal who didn't know sign language. She got what she wanted by holding her breath until she turned blue. In those days, the deaf were considered mentally defective. She was thought of as "a poor unfortunate." She scrubbed the floors of the institution to pay the state back. When she got scarlet fever, they put her in a little room in the basement for several weeks. She was learning to be a stoic.

My father was born in rural Alabama. He was struck by lightning when he was four. His mother died when he was twelve. He didn't understand that she had died; he had never seen a dead person before. He saw her, his best friend, lying still in a pine box, in the back of a wagon pulled by a mule. He nudged his father and told him that she was cold. He did not comprehend death.

Right after his mother died, his father took him on a train ride. He was happy, excited, a little country bumpkin called "Buddy." Then they walked into this strange building, the institution [State School for the Deaf in Talladega, Alabama], and all his father said to him was: "I'm going to leave you here."

I remember what my father told me about that turning point in his life: "I turned around and he was gone." I remember when my father took me to an Episcopal school, he went to pieces. We kissed good-bye and I watched him walk away from the dormitory. I could tell from the back of his body that he was crying. I never knew why until he told me the story.

I went to college on scholarship, and twice a year I'd have to go to see the bishop to get my check. At the end of every meeting, the bishop rose from his chair, put his arm around me and said: "Remember who you are, what you represent."

That idea was always ringing in my ears. He meant I am their daughter, that they are the best example of goodness I can imagine. This is something I cannot, do not, forget. It colors everything I do. I am a mixture of them. My legacy is that their bad handicap has not been bad. Deafness was not the main thing about them. The main thing was that their major compulsion was living. They assimilated into the hearing world. They got into the mainstream. They weren't stopped by deafness. They did it despite their deafness.

Princess
Yasmin Aga Khan

on being a daughter

My mother used to call me "Dolly." Not everyday. Just on special occasions. The occasions had less to do with holidays than with ordinary moments that were their own beacons of light.

When a shining moment became an event that marked our journey together, she would refer to me as "Dolly." When she did, I knew that in her heart I had measured up to something beyond dearest. We understood the depth of the "Dolly" conversational shorthand, the specialness of it, because my mother used love words infrequently. She often kissed me with her eyes and, although her silent sign of affection satisfied me, there was nothing quite as wonderful as being referred to as "Dolly."

She referred to me that way every time I won a major journalism prize. When the time between prizes seemed too widely spaced, she'd say: "Dolly, I dreamed you won a prize," and, within days, I really had. She used that word when I got a raise or a promotion or if I looked good. She used it when I painted a picture she liked or when I played her a song on the piano when the snow was falling.

The year she was sick and dying, when I became her eyes and ears at the hospital, her voice with the surgeons, her helper in all things, she seemed to forget the ultimate word of affection. She was too weak, too sick, too involved with coming to terms with her impending death and not burdening me with her own fears to use the word.

When she could still speak, not a whole comprehensible sentence, but a word here and there, I asked her if she wanted something. One blink was yes. Two blinks were no. There was one blink. After a string of yes's and no's using the blink method, it turned out that she wanted her portable radio next to her hospital bed. She didn't have the strength to operate the on-off button. What she wanted, really, was to be surrounded by familiar things. When I brought her the radio, I said to her: "Here it is, Mom. Did I ever let you down?"

I asked the question jocularly, expecting nothing more than two blinks.

Summoning every shred of energy in her cancer-wasted body, she whispered two words which became my greatest source of comfort when she joined the absent: "No, Dolly." I knew she was talking not of the radio but about the quality of our life together. Her last words have lasted forever.

When I interviewed Princess Yasmin Aga Khan in her lavish New York apartment, we spoke about our mothers and what it took to be a supportive daughter in times of great pain and sorrow. I told Princess Yasmin my "Dolly" story concisely, in a sentence or two. She told me about her relationship with her late mother, the movie star Rita Hayworth who, at the height of her career, married her father, Prince Aly Khan.

The Princess and her mother were close and she, too, watched her mother die, from the ravages of Alzheimer's. We shared the commonalities of our experience as our mothers' primary caretakers, then the Princess told me what it was like for her.

    Alzheimer's disease leads to senility. It also leads to loss of dignity. My mother had always been very conscious of herself. She always ate correctly and had excellent manners. Then she became incontinent. She couldn't even speak. All she could do was mumble-jumble.

I was devoted to my mother. It was a natural feeling. She

had an incredible career. But she also had difficulties.

My mother denied the painful realities of her sickness by turning to alcohol. She became fearful. She drank herself sick. Her liver was swollen. By the time she was diagnosed as having Alzheimer's, she was too far gone to really understand what was happening to her.

She was losing her memory. She tried to hang on for dear life. I wish I could have helped her sooner. I wish she had said to me, "Help! I'm drowning!" I wish I could have found her the right doctor. That's what I regret. Not being able to do enough for her.

She had outbursts of rage. She didn't understand her awkward behavior. I wish I could have helped her get it under control so that she didn't embarrass herself. Or me. And she did. Oh, yes, I'm scared about inheriting the disease. If my mind gets blocked, I think, "Oh, God, I've got the beginnings of Alzheimer's." If I have difficulty expressing myself, my reaction is the same.

My mother was witty. She wasn't either a trickster or someone who dealt in malicious practical jokes. But she could laugh when things went wrong.

She tried to hide the fact that senility was setting in, that she couldn't remember the name of her hotel or how to count to 10 or who was president of the United States. She'd giggle and go on to something else.

I'm self-conscious about Alzheimer's. I don't want to be a burden to anyone. I'd want to pull the plug. I know how hard it is for the victim and the caretaker. I watched her go through the stages of her illness, the regressions. I felt helpless. I didn't want to institutionalize her. But the question always was: When is she really going to fall apart? It was like walking on eggshells.

There were times she was miserable and I knew it. And she knew that I knew. If she was in a personal relationship that wasn't working for her, she didn't share that with me. But even then, I felt for her. I understood. Sometimes she would lash out in anger at me, or at anyone. But I considered that a passing storm. She was frustrated.

When I was eight, she had me brought to her movie set to watch her performance. She was so magnificent-looking. She could always transform herself into the character she played. When I saw her act, she seemed a hundred times bigger than her real self.

Later, at home, there she was in her bathrobe and slippers. We would swim in the pool together. She never let her public image interfere with our relationship.

Then she got sick.

The breakup of her marriage to my father had a major impact on her. Then my father died when I was 10. Psychologically, their separation, their divorce and then his death hit her badly. Her equilibrium was out of balance. She was jolted and it made her susceptible to illness. Alzheimer's set in, only we didn't know it was Alzheimer's. What I know is that if you're severely disturbed emotionally, you can become severely disturbed physically.

There were times I thought I couldn't cope. I felt bombarded. During the most intense times, I was supported by an old friend, a psychologist. I talked to him. I discussed my feelings. I tried to understand myself and my mother's condition.

That's how I found the strength to go on. It was a fight on my part. I brought my will into focus. I've had a fairly easy life. The challenge for me was to do as much as I could for my mother so that later, when it was time for me to die, I would feel peaceful about my efforts.

Queen Noor

on life's demands

Queen Noor of Jordan walks tall and straight.

I waited a long time to see that gait. Almost two hours, in fact.

An interview had been set and confirmed. I had been cleared by the State Department. At the appointed time, I was where I was supposed to be: seated in the reception area of a lavish suite in Boston's Ritz-Carlton hotel. I could hear the reverberations of rambunctious children playing, giggling, stomping somewhere beyond closed doors in the immediate distance. Later, out of the tangle of voices that rose from the overheard babble, I would recognize a voice that was both distinctly American and tantalizingly sweet. It was the Queen's.

The Queen's extension of the "continental one hour late" excuse had to do with her children. My interview time had obviously clashed with their play time, and that's something the Queen wouldn't relinquish.

Still: there was a an esoteric sign that the Queen, who shuns extended personal interviews, would appear. The sign took a human form—a short, wiry dark-skinned man in a business suit, obviously a security guard, who stood at attention at the other side of the door. I knew he was there because, from time to time, he opened the door, shot a glance in my direction and, before closing the door and disappearing again, announced: "The Queen will arrive." He didn't say when. The wait was about a leap in faith.

Finally the door opened and the Queen appeared.

She is movie-star beautiful, a Washington-born American who is a graduate of Princeton. The first hour had been whiled away with her children. She was an American talking to an American and she apologized swiftly but gracefully. The second hour delay needed no explanation. It had obviously been devoted to grooming herself for the photographer at my side. Her long blonde hair, meticulously streaked with subtle flashes of vanilla ice cream, had been brushed and coiffed to perfection. Her flawless silk daisy-print wrap dress had no wrinkles. Her make-up was a cosmetic director's dream. Every eyelash seemed to have been mascara-brushed one by one, slowly and meticulously. Her lipstick had been drawn on by an artist using a sable brush.

I understood the necessity for the guard at the door, a subtle personification of the palace guard mentality. The palace we were in, the palace beyond The Palace in Jordan, could have been viewed by fanatics as a killing field. How easy to start anew the Mideast war by an attack on the family of King Hussein.

The Queen addressed the possibility of the assassination of King Hussein realistically. She now faces the possibility of the King's death by a different kind of enemy: B-cell lymphoma. As I write, he is undergoing chemotherapy at the Mayo Clinic in Rochester, Minnesota.

Queen Noor, whose name means "light" in Arabic, is the former Lisa Halaby. Before her marriage, her first and the King's fourth, she had been a design director for Alia, the Royal Jordanian Airline in Amman. Her father, Najeeb Halaby, the son of a Syrian immigrant, had been president and chairman of Pan American World Airways (1969-1972).

When Queen Noor married King Hussein, she converted from Protestantism to Islam. She relinquished her American citizenship. She gladly assumed a new job: an American Queen in Amman, a thoroughly modern spokesperson in the Muslim world where women are forced to shroud themselves in black.

We spoke about the demands of her life and on her life. She didn't hold back.

When the King and I committed ourselves to each other, it felt right. I felt as if destiny had stepped in and taken over, that there was finally meaning to all the previous actions of my life. I continued to feel that way. There's so much the King and I can do together. I pray for my husband's life. I also pray for his long life, his health, his happiness.

Of course I could be filled with fear about an assassination. That kind of thinking would cripple me. It would inhibit me. So I try to put such notions out of my mind. I've learned, through experience, that there are many dimensions of the spirit and that we must be discriminating and choose a productive path. I don't like to be sidetracked. So I try not to think of the King's dangers. Sometimes I succeed.

I'm not heroic. I'm foolhardy. I've simply assumed my responsibilies by virtue of my birth and my marriage. I'm putting myself to use. My life demands that. My husband has sacrificed so much for his country. He would have liked an unstructured period in his life. But he was handed responsibility early. The problems have not receded for my husband. They've multiplied. As time passes, we're further from a Mideast solution. The King needs me. I feel I must be there to comfort him, even in menial ways. That's not a humbling of pride. I've made a commitment to the man I love.

One word that describes my husband best is "inspiration." He has inspired me to give more of myself, to know more about myself. There's a difference in our age. But we have bonded. There has been a synthesis. Under all the demands made on us, if it weren't for those shared feelings of love, I would not have been able to cope, to continue to believe that the struggle is worthwhile.

Yes, I'm speaking of the political struggle of the Mideast. That struggle is behind everything in our lives. There is no vacation from it. We're dedicated to peace in our area. I'm crusading for peace. I believe peace is of interest to everybody.

Americans, Arabs and Israelis. My husband and I share the struggle for peace. It's one of the things that has unified us. For my husband, my children, for everyone, peace would be a miraculous blessing. It would also be an affirmation of faith in humanity. Some people work to acquire wealth. We are working to acquire peace. Peace is the greatest wealth.

I am sensitive to traditions. Yes, I am a sister in spirit, as well as activity, to the women in my country. I try to explain things to them in my way. I am trying, also, to broaden relations between Jordan and other countries around the world.

Feminism is not a term I use. But I am a great promoter of opportunities for women in my country. I set an example for women to take advantage of an opportunity. I want women to express themselves outside the traditional role of motherhood. The family is a unified element, an important one, the base of every society. But women can get beyond that.

Maria Cole

on making choices

Maria Cole relinquished her musical career to promote her husband's musical career.

That was a choice.

It is not widely known that she had dropped out of a clerical school to sing with orchestras in Boston and then in New York, including the Duke Ellington Band. She was rehearsing at New York's Zanzibar Club when Nat King Cole dropped in, took one look and asked: "Who's that?" Ten months later they were married. Whatever road he took, she took. They walked side by side.

That was a choice.

Maria Cole raised five children, including the singer Natalie Cole. She was also her husband's bookkeeper and the person who coordinated his complicated schedule which she negotiated with his agent. When they'd been married about ten years, she was chagrined to see women flirt openly with her husband and his delight in it. She conquered her anxieties by reinventing herself. She created her own nightclub act and starred in it. She was a knockout. Maria had abandoned showcasing her talents to promote his, but she showed Nat that she could re-instigate her own career at any time.

That was a choice.

Ultimately, she returned to her husband's side, his trail, his bookings. She painstakingly continued to promote his career, not hers. She gave Nat King Cole her priority time, her priority attention, her priority energy. Her children weren't exactly ecstatic about their mother's escalating absence. But even the children's criticisms, which still echo, couldn't pull Maria from Nat.

That was a choice.

Maria Cole, a postman's daughter, now lives in a spectacular luxury apartment located in a Brahmin bastion overlooking the spectacular manicured gardens of Boston Common. We got together there to talk about the choices she had made.

She is strong in her opinions. She talks slowly, deliberately, carefully weighing her words and the impact of the ideas behind them. Her concept of choice suggests that when you make a decision, you use all the information you have at hand, and proceed logically. However: your emotions are a governing force and sometimes that way you feel about the options overshadows and overwhelms what you think.

When it came to Nat King Cole, she followed her heart. That's the thing about believing in the rightness of your choices. You respect the liberty of having chosen for yourself rather than having a choice thrust at you. That's a good thing. Maria does not regret the routes on which she embarked. She always got what she wanted: results.

    My children had a celebrity father. That reality influenced their lives enormously. He was famous. I loved my husband so much that I spent all my time with him.

    I regret that I didn't realize the seriousness of that decision. I wanted to be with him. My children have blamed me for this for years. When anything goes wrong, they still say: "It's because Mom wasn't there." Nat wanted to improve himself. He did not come from a privileged background. And I wanted to help him improve. What he needed, I had. What I needed, he had. That's why our marriage worked.

    I was very involved in his life. I dealt with his agent. I kept his books. I was there for all the wonderful moments of his life, the accolades. We shared everything. I merged into his life.

Ten years into our marriage, I saw women openly flirting with him. One day he said: "Why don't you go home and stay with the kids for two weeks?" How would you feel? A wife knows what a husband means when he says things like that. I died inside. Eventually, I was able to tell him how I felt. He denied my fears.

It was then I acknowledged a need to prove myself to myself. I wanted to prove that I could be important, that I could be successful, that I could be respected. I didn't want to be known only as Mrs. Nat King Cole. I wanted to be me.

I got an act together and performed at Ciro's in Los Angeles. When I got applause, Nat cried. I didn't see him cry. I was on stage. My sister was there, and she told me. I knew that I had proven the point to both of us. I didn't feel revenge. I just felt good.

I learned many things from Nat. One of the most important things he taught me was tolerance. I was always impatient. He made excuses for people. He'd say, "I know it happened, but ..." He always considered the "buts."

I miss the closeness of my marriage to Nat. I loved hearing his key in the door. I loved preparing his meals. I loved being married to him.

Yes, I'd get married again, but I need a secure man who is a doer. Even when Nat was home and not supposed to be working, he was at the piano. His world was his work and his work was his world.

Creativity is innate. His creativity was always on the surface. That's a doer.

Our daughter Natalie had a drug problem. She was a grown woman on her own, and I didn't know anything about it. She didn't want to deal with it. Finally, she said, "I'm ready." But she was almost dead. I was naïve. I thought I knew it all. I didn't know a thing about drugs.

I was visiting in her home. I saw straws in the bathroom. I told her valet that she needed a new maid, that the house was messy. The valet, a family friend, took me aside and said: "That's how they freebase." My daughter has taken herself in hand now. She's had therapy. She blamed me for everything. It goes back to what I told you before. I spent my time with my husband.

My personality is strong. I'm independent. I've been criticized for being so independent. In my generation, independence was considered a flaw. I've been traumatized by that. I still question my independence.

Nat was the first black artist to have a television show. It was 1957 and he could attract only one sponsor. He made a classic statement then. He said, "Madison Avenue is afraid of the dark."

He was sad, hurt, and mortified. I was furious. I felt defeat. He felt defeat. But he went on. He continued. He had hit after hit. That was the best revenge. That's what I think about now when I think of him.

Ann Landers

on things happening for the best

A uniformed butler bowed slightly, his chin up, and waved me into this version of an American palace. He informed me in almost-clipped British tones that "The Madam"—that's what he called the lady of the magnificent house—would join me momentarily. He wasn't exactly Masterpiece Theatre. But close.

This is the best of Chicago, the finest address in town. I am standing in a living room of a sprawling antique-filled apartment, looking down at a placid Lake Michigan through a spotless window that's nearly the length and height of an entire wall. The remaining paneled walls are studded with fine art. The furniture is a chic mix of beige contemporary and brocaded Louis XVI.

It's early afternoon. I'm waiting for The Madam to arrive. Her name is Ann Landers and, although her advice column is syndicated to 1,200 newspapers, this is not a place built strictly on a career in newspapering. Landers, who was married for 36 years to Jules W. Lederer, the founder of Budget Rent-A-Car, received a nice settlement when they were divorced.

We'd met before. But her life had changed radically, and suddenly, and she agreed to a second interview. She had left the *Chicago Sun-Times*, after 33 years, to go with the rival *Chicago Tribune*. The professional change, paired with being single again, suggested that perhaps she had some advice about what you do when life starts playing tricks on you and you happen to be in your seventies.

The palace had been as quiet as a tomb. I could hear a clock ticking somewhere. But I couldn't even hear the traffic down below. What I finally heard was a steady swish, the click of heels on a parquet floor before the step was muffled by the thick carpet. I smelled fine perfume, Hermés, I think, perhaps Calèche.

I turned around and there was Ann Landers, in a long satin dressing gown that could have doubled for a black tie event. She was carefully coiffed, carefully manicured, professionally made-up and smiling as she made a grand entrance. So this is how newspaper women looked when they worked at home! Landers, who's from Sioux City, Iowa, maintained an office down the hall.

In her wake was a uniformed maid carrying a tea tray that included warm scones filled with chocolate. The tray was set for three. Landers had expected a photographer. My editors, who had decided against investing in new pictures, lost a wonderful opportunity. Ann Landers was the most untypical newspaper woman I have ever seen in my life. She was dressed for a party.

That was, in fact, the underlying tenor of the interview. She believed that when bad things happen, you examine them, understand them, and accept them. If you can do all that, and she believes you can, you might as well celebrate as you get on with it. That's what she was doing: celebrating. So we ate chocolate scones and drank tea, and the anchor of advice said what was on her mind.

I never felt ditched by my husband. He gave us both the opportunity to have a better life. The divorce was a good thing. It's easy to be friendly with my ex-husband because I'm not bitter.

When the marriage broke up, I wasn't a wreck. I knew I'd be fine. I knew he'd be fine. I didn't lose a night's sleep over the situation. My husband got involved with a much younger woman. They're married now. It did work out fine.

Life is one damn thing after another. Life is a roller coaster ride. It's not what happens to you but how you handle what happens to you. Are you going to lie down and die? Are you going to be angry and bitter?

It's better to accept the problem, look at it as a challenge. The minute you start figuring out ways to solve a situation, you're involved in a learning experience.

But when I got married, it never occurred to me that I'd be unmarried. I thought I was married for life. Now I wouldn't marry again for anything. I am enjoying my freedom.

I'm seeing three different men now. One is much younger. I invited him to a trip to Morocco. Our party host, Malcolm Forbes, suggested we share a room. "It's okay," he said. "Well, it's not okay with me," I said!

I'm also seeing an older man, someone very intelligent. And I'm seeing a man who's a little younger than me. All the men I date are good dancers. I like to be with a man who dances.

It's absolutely possible to have a successful platonic relationship with a man. What's going on is cerebral, not sexual. The relationship requires something in common with the man. You need things to talk about. A man has to know what interests the woman. And she should be able to listen.

I haven't been fighting in the front lines of feminism. The less shrill feminist appeals to me. She doesn't draw the fire the screamers and yellers draw. Screamers and yellers look crazy. They look out of control. I prefer to state my position forcefully—and leave it at that.

Feminists don't like the word *lady*. When I use the word, I mean a woman who is cultured and refined as opposed to a tough broad. The ladies are more effective because people are more inclined to listen to them. They talk sense. It's a difference in presentation. When your presentation is not appealing, you hurt your cause.

I get a lot of letters. The ones that touch me the most are

from simple, ordinary people who are heroes but don't call themselves heroes. They are people who have demanding, restrictive lives. They accept their fate. They accept situations that I would consider disasters. But they go on, day after day, without complaining. They don't say: "Why me?" I look at these people as noble.

I don't get many crackpot letters, you know, nut mail. My column has improved. I used to write superficially. My work was much less substantive. I'm not as funny as I used to be either. I've matured. I realize that people who write to me seriously have no place else to go. That's a sobering thought.

I know I've got critics. I feel they're entitled to their opinion. If they don't think I'm good, fine. I think I'm good. My opinion is more important than theirs.

I wasn't born with confidence. I've developed my confidence. Success is what gives you confidence. Failure makes you unsure of yourself. You wonder if something is wrong with you. You question your judgments.

Then your uncertainty shows. If a person has too many failures in life, that person needs counseling. People have to talk out their failures. They have to understand what went wrong. Once you understand the "why" of a failure, you move on.

I've been called the voice of reason. I can look at a situation, see both sides and decide where I stand. That's the voice of reason. It's the opposite of the voice of emotion. I think things through rather than feel things through.

I was with the *Chicago Sun-Times* for thirty-three years when Rupert Murdoch took over. That was a problem. I was beyond retirement age. I'd been there a long time. Should I leave the security or go to a new paper? It looked as if leaving was a risky thing to do.

In the end, I decided to leave on the basis of a principle. "Was it an honorable move? Was I going to improve my work?" My answer to myself was: "Yes! yes!"

Life gets easier as you get older. I don't let anybody push me around or tell me what to do. I'm selective with my time and energy. Sometimes I think: "Everybody wants a little piece of me and there's not so much of me to go around." So I just say "no."

I don't see a reason to retire. That would be a crazy thing to do. I love my work. I'm at the top of my game. I'm going to die on the job. At age eighty-eight, I'm just going to slump over my typewriter. That will be it.

Olympia Dukakis

on aging

They didn't make Olympia Dukakis a big star until she was in her sixties, until she won an Oscar for her role in *Moonstruck*. Dukakis, a first-generation American, is vociferous about the fact that it took so long, too long, for her to reach the top.

All her life she has fought stereotypes. One was the burden of a Greek name, not exactly saleable in Hollywood circles. Another was her age. Hollywood doesn't glorify older women. But Dukakis has neither changed her name nor surgically altered her appearance in a dramatic way.

We are sitting together in the atrium of The Ten Park Restaurant, an ordinary neighborhood bistro in Montclair, New Jersey, in the shadow of Dukakis' house. The place seems deserted. But I later discover that the owners had closed off the atrium so that it became Dukakis' exclusive domain, a sort of substitute executive office. Very nice, I say. Very late, she says. What she means is that her celebrity, and its fruits, are a little tardy. Her left eyebrow shoots up in a comic sneer and she deadpans: "Better late than never."

Whatever demeans older women is what Dukakis demeans.

Despite her stellar accomplishments, the world tends to look at her the way it looks at all older women: as "used-up rather than filled-up." She winces in righteous indignation.

Her firebrand presence, a blend of misfit and maverick, commands respect. When she doesn't get it, she becomes vocal. She argues. She even raises her voice. She states her case. Dukakis says that's the good side of Aging. You don't swallow your pride. You flaunt it.

Dukakis, who dotes on salad diets, has traveled a long and trouble-infested road personally and professionally. She says that she knows exactly how she survived setbacks, how she activated her career toward stardom. All good things started when she began to think of herself not as an old crone but, simply, as a crone.

Impossible! Dukakis isn't a cantankerous, ugly, old hag. Impossible! She is not a crone.

Yet Dukakis, who has a gift of description, said she turns the word *crone* into a softer, kinder, more elegant version than Webster's dictionary.

A crone, according to Dukakis, is an older woman who has come to an understanding of herself and her life. A crone is willing to make substitutes. She understands that life is cyclical, that it has seasons, and that in order for something new to grow, something old has to pass away. She accepts that reality with grace but never in silence. Chin up, shoulders lowered, her gaze steady, Dukakis, a woman of presence, spoke vividly about the specific milestones that, cumulatively, made her the crone she is.

    We see older people as used-up rather than filled-up. We don't talk about their accumulated experiences. We talk about their accumulated years. We even say: "She is such-and-such an age, but look at how young she looks."

An old word, "crone," is coming into new use. It now refers to the older person who has come to an understanding of herself and her life.

I see myself becoming a crone.

Now, more than ever, I am focused on my spiritual journey. A spiritual journey is a quest that puts you at one with life. It's the opposite of being at odds with life. I don't need approval the way I did before. I always had to feel I was doing the right thing. I always worried that I might be doing the wrong thing.

Now I think success and failure have the same common denominator. They are for learning. What you take from your trials is the same basic thing you take from your success—a lesson.

I used to find it difficult to enjoy my success. I couldn't relax. I was always on-guard and watchful. I didn't feel pleased and satisfied. It all culminated around the events of *Moonstruck*. I actually downplayed that success.

I thought: "But what about all the other parts I've done?" Then a friend said something important to me. "All your work shows in *Moonstruck*. It's all there." The understanding of that was a gift.

People who behave in an autocratic, imperial way make me volatile. Whatever it is, I communicate it in an expressive way. I try to be judicious about my volatility. I'm a proud person. Probably too proud.

I was told early on in my career to change my name. I was warned I'd be typecast. Look at me! Look! If you didn't know my name, don't you think I could look like a Mary Johnson? Of course I could pass for Mary Johnson! You bet! But with a name like Dukakis, a lot of producers wouldn't even see me or let me audition. They even assumed I was born in Greece! For a long time, I felt like an outsider because of my name. I felt shut out. I felt I would not have the opportunity to do what I was capable of doing. I had fought a lot in street fights over my name ... many times I was beat up or did some beating on my own. I was called "greaseball." The kids made fun of me because I'm Greek.

My immigrant father hoped his daughter wouldn't have to struggle. I remember once he came into a little theater on Charles Street in Boston, and there I was, working with everyone there, moving furniture and painting sets. I was just out of Boston University. He stood there, tears in his eyes, and said: "I've worked all my life to save you from this."

But my father also knew that life is about jumping in, rather than being saved from the struggle. Children of immigrant parents don't take opportunities for granted. They fight for them, and that's the struggle. He knew I wanted to be a real part of the times in which I lived.

My husband had a terrible auto accident. He was out of commission for three years. To this day, he wears a brace. We had mortgage payments to make, so I worked at whatever acting jobs I could get. But, first, I had to accept my situation. One day, when I was alone in the kitchen, I sat at our table, put my head on my arms and said: "Things are never going to be the same again." One I understood that, I made plans.

I had a master calendar on which I organized everything for everyone in the family. I prioritized. Organization is helpful when your life becomes messed up.

When my husband got well, he couldn't get any work. That was another kind of paralysis, career paralysis. He had moods and that created problems at home.

My daughter cut classes. She stayed out later. I found liquor in her purse. We had to go to family therapy. It turned out that the person who actually had the problem was me. I still operated from a crisis mentality. I had to understand that my husband was not a patient anymore. I had to understand that I didn't need a calendar anymore. I didn't have to organize everybody's life to the last details.

Now my daughter and I are good friends. Then her rebellion was incisive. Her actions were exact. What she said about me, about her father, about our life was painful. It was not what I wanted to hear. She went to great lengths to wake me up. I talk plainly. She talked plainly. In terms of strength, she matched me toe-to-toe. The things she said were all true. So I let go. It was because of her honesty that I began to change and to grow ... I began to relax.

Overnight celebrity is a romantic notion. In my case, it just isn't true. I've worked as an actor for twenty years. It took a while for me to learn my trade. Maybe life is destined. I have a fateful attitude. Things are meant to happen when they happen.

I'm overly ambitious. So I place limits on myself. I tend to see more and want to do more than I can handle. My husband has taught me how to cope. He says: "Just take the next single, simple step." Now, I try to think only of today. I used to try to do everything in one day.

For a long time, I felt like an outsider because of my name. I felt shut out. I felt I would not have the opportunity to do what I was capable of doing. I wanted to play great parts and work with wonderful people.

It's still what I want.

Epilogue

I was a million years away from the magic of computers or, in fact, any magic at all.

I worked full time filing ink-stained Addressograph Plates which were inserted into a machine that addressed envelopes automatically. The man in charge of the state-of-the-art operation, staged in a windowless dingy-dirty government stockroom, didn't care in what order the plates went into the machine. He cared only that the file drawers were in perfect alphabetical order. If they weren't, an inspector might rate him low on his sense of organization.

What made the job bearable is that I studied journalism at night at Boston University. I paid for my tuition and textbooks from my meager pay. There was no budget for an adequate supper before evening classes. So I existed on tea and toast, a regular feast for many years, twenty cents total. The tea was a symbolic elixir. It sustained me. Life was sweet. If my father had any suspicions, he didn't let on. Maybe it was because I even managed to pay room and board. I was beginning to be of some value to him.

Yet there was a hitch. It was not unusual then for lovesick teenagers to plot furtive getaways to keep romantic after-dark trysts. My problem involved sneaking unobserved *into* the house after evening classes, floating to my room on a cloud of silence (and victory!) without being seen or heard. My mother, who had secretly sanctioned what was forbidden to me, homework rather than housework, was my co-conspirator. We formed a kind of mother-daughter alliance, a primitive form of networking that feminists refer to as the "sisterhood." Subversiveness had replaced subservience.

Evenings when I wasn't around, my mother told my father that I was working overtime. In the broad sense, it was the absolute truth. I arrived from evening classes after ten o'clock in the evening several nights a week. My father watched television, sometimes snoozing, and I eased quietly into my room. If he was half-awake, and my mother heard my key in the lock, she distracted him by talking about whatever was happening on the small screen. Her plotted cover-ups allowed me to continue on the journalistic journey that finally, after decades of interviewing, has brought me to the threshold of this book.

There is no reason to have shared this secret duress and, then again, there is every reason. No reason because I never intended to make this book even slightly autobiographical, and every reason because my one-woman war was far less solitary, far less lonely than I imagined.

How I opened my own door to journalism is the key to how I skipped past an editorial STOP sign to change ordinary interviews, with the constancy of their looming deadlines, into oral history. How I ultimately discovered that obstacles of every sort are a woman's legacy, and so is her innate ability to unravel and thus resolve them, is linked to how I nudged the interview process beyond the inhibiting facade of celebrity and amassed an intimate personal diary of prefeminist life. Because I was obsessed to know how other older, wiser women, like you and like me, got from where they were to where they wanted to be, is how this book was born.

All these "hows" intersected my consciousness like an overview of electrified crisscross landscape glimpsed from an airplane in a nighttime descent. When, on a personal whim, I retraveled the sum total of my work, which includes many famous men, the clarity of hindsight made certain famous female voices jump out of the chorus and crescendo into a sweeping oratorio of prefeminist life. One single theory underlines and dominates the undercurrents of this diary: Conformity is the enemy of originality.

Every time my father cut me off, every time he equated conformity with obedience, I condemned conformity as relinquishing my creativity, denying the inner core of my true self. Every woman who has ever stumbled into the unfairness of an unreasonable STOP sign, with all its demeaning connotations, knows that conformity and no-no's go together.

For a woman, the "cannot" territory is endless. I wandered into prohibited "cannot" territory when, at a crest of my newspaper career, I proposed that celebrity interviews could assume futuristic significance if presented to the reader as oral history: Famous people talking about their innermost secrets in the first person.

Hahaha, said my legendary editor, Tom Winship, after I wrote my first experimental all-quotes story with a brief introduction. In fact, sounding like an echo of my father, he issued a warning: "You cannot do this on a regular basis. You cannot expect people to talk to you like this all the time." It was as if I was seventeen again. Stopped again. In a one-woman war again.

Only this time I was lucky. I was talking with the father of my career, a fine editor, who let me express my instincts, my ideas, my feelings, my sureness that if, in the writing of my story I stepped out of it entirely, people would understand that what they were reading was not stream-of-consciousness but a melange of quotes that, during the writing process, I wove together like tapestry. These quotes resulted from an intense exchange, often emotional, and they had the truth of immediacy.

There was no guarantee that all the famous people that I would be assigned to interview from then on, would collaborate willingly with me, a by-liner taking notes of questions layered in more questions. Still I wanted to pioneer the interview into new territory, into a "conversation" akin to what goes on in a session with a trusted psychiatrist. I wanted to reveal the unrevealed, to challenge, cajole and compare experiences about the inner life. I wanted to do this within the sphere of patience, courtesy and the kind of innate goodwill that made people gravitate toward my mother.

That's what I was thinking when Winship shattered my reverie by posing a question of compromise. "If I let you do this, and I think you cannot, will you be a big enough person to come into my office and say: 'I've failed'?"

It was daunting.

But it didn't eclipse my overwhelming desire to see and hear, up close and personal, the army of underrated prefeminists who fought their battles alone, put illuminating clues into the ordinary and paved the way for the feminist movement as we now know it.

I now see that my professional destiny has come full circle. When I worked in the stockroom and studied journalism at night, I used my lunchtime breaks to peddle stories to Tom Winship's father, Larry Winship, also a *Boston Globe* editor. The elder Winship paid ten dollars per story. That, in addition to my minuscule government pay, made it possible for me to buy secondhand reference books, advance my father room and board and not starve. I had money left over for tea and toast suppers. Neither Winship ever knew any of this.

On the day I asked to make the oral history of famous people a regular journalistic format, I told Tom Winship that I would not fail, that I'd make him proud. He said we should seal the bargain with something liquid. It was late morning. He offered coffee. I asked for tea. What transpired next gave me a sense of closure and confidence. He buzzed his secretary and, over the intercom, announced: "Tea for Two."

About the Author

Marian Christy, most recently the Media Director of Special Collections at Boston University, has been a frequent contributor to The New York Times Syndicate. She was the recipient of 30 prestigious journalism awards during her 26-year tenure as an editor and top Boston Globe syndicated columnist (1965-1991). She is the only three-time winner of the University of Missouri Journalism's J.C. Penney Awards (1966-1968-1970).

When Christy took an early retirement from the *Boston Globe* (November 1991), she was asked to write and host The Monitor Channel's *Lifestyles With Marian Christy* television program. She signed a three-year contract. The Monitor Channel went black in April 1992.

Cosmopolitan Magazine, in 1979, honored Christy as one of America's five top American journalists. She is the author of the critically-acclaimed book *Invasions of Privacy: Notes from a Celebrity Journalist,* an insider's look at the real world of newspapering. Christy is working on the manuscript of a third book.

Christy joined the *Boston Globe* as the Fashion Editor in 1965 after a distinguished career with the New York-based Fairchild Publications where she wrote features for *Women's Wear Daily.* Her first *Globe* assignments were in Europe, where she wrote reports and editorials from the major couture salons in Paris, Rome, Madrid, Barcelona, Athens, Dublin and London.

She completed elective studies at Harvard University Extension School and earned a Certificate in Journalism from Boston University (1965) by working days and studying evenings. Her first job was working as a file clerk in a government stockroom. She was awarded a "Distinguished Alumni Award" for standards of excellence in journalism from Boston University's College of Communication (1985). Her papers are included in the internationally-prestigious Boston University 20th Century Archives Collection.

In 1987 she was awarded an Honorary Doctorate of Humane Letters from Franklin Pierce College, Rindge, New Hampshire.

Christy switched to celebrity journalism in 1981 and created the original, and now much imitated, "Conversations" approach to question-and-answer interviews. Her work has become a unique pioneering study in oral history as a journalism style. It is based on intimate one-on-one talks with highly achieved people from a wide variety of fields. She is well known for her ability to penetrate the veneer and get to the heart and mind of her world-famous subjects.

Marian Christy is quoted in such books as: William Wright's *Claus Von Bulow*; in Lester David's *Joan:The Reluctant Kennedy*; in Julie Nixon Eisenhower's book on her mother, Pat Nixon; in Camelia Sadat's autobiography which focuses on her late father, the Egyptian president, Anwar Sadat; in David Sinclair's book *Snowdon*, about Lord Snowdon; and at length in Alan Gerson's book *The Kirkpatrick Mission* (Jeanne Kirkpatrick, then head of the U.S. Mission to the U.N.).